D1073740

THE WILLS
OF OUR
ANCESTORS

DATE DUE

FAMILY HISTORY FROM PEN & SWORD

Birth, Marriage and Death Records
David Annal and Audrey Collins

Tracing Your Channel Islands Ancestors
Marie-Louise Backhurst

Tracing Your Yorkshire Ancestors
Rachel Bellerby

The Great War Handbook
Geoff Bridger

Tracing Your Royal Marine Ancestors
Richard Brooks and Matthew Little

Your Rural Ancestors
Jonathan Brown

Tracing Your Pauper Ancestors
Robert Burlison

Tracing Your Huguenot Ancestors
Kathy Chater

Tracing Your East End Ancestors
Jane Cox

Tracing Your Labour Movement Ancestors
Mark Crail

Tracing Your Ancestors
Simon Fowler

Tracing Your Army Ancestors
Simon Fowler

A Guide to Military History on the Internet
Simon Fowler

Tracing Your Northern Ancestors
Keith Gregson

Your Irish Ancestors
Ian Maxwell

Tracing Your Northern Irish Ancestors
Ian Maxwell

Tracing Your Scottish Ancestors
Ian Maxwell

Tracing Your London Ancestors
Jonathan Oates

Tracing Family History on the Internet
Christopher Patton

Tracing Your Prisoner of War Ancestors: The First World War
Sarah Paterson

Tracing Your Tank Ancestors
Janice Tait and David Fletcher

Great War Lives
Paul Reed

Tracing Your Air Force Ancestors
Phil Tomaselli

Tracing Your Second World War Ancestors
Phil Tomaselli

Tracing Your Secret Service Ancestors
Phil Tomaselli

Tracing Your Criminal Ancestors
Stephen Wade

Tracing Your Legal Ancestors
Stephen Wade

Tracing Your Police Ancestors
Stephen Wade

Tracing Your Jewish Ancestors
Rosemary Wenzerul

Fishing and Fishermen
Martin Wilcox

Tracing Your Canal Ancestors
Sue Wilkes

Tracing Your Lancashire Ancestors
Sue Wilkes

THE WILLS
OF OUR
ANCESTORS

A Guide to Probate Records for
Family and Local Historians

Stuart A. Raymond

Pen & Sword
FAMILY HISTORY

First published in Great Britain in 2012 by
PEN & SWORD FAMILY HISTORY
An imprint of
Pen & Sword Books Ltd
47 Church Street
Barnsley
South Yorkshire
S70 2AS

ISBN 978-1-84884-785-9

Typeset by Concept, Huddersfield, West Yorkshire.
Printed and bound in England by CPI Group (UK) Ltd, Croydon, CR0 4YY.

Pen & Sword Books Ltd incorporates the imprints of
Pen & Sword Aviation, Pen & Sword Family History, Pen & Sword Maritime,
Pen & Sword Military, Pen & Sword Discovery, Wharncliffe Local History,
Wharncliffe True Crime, Wharncliffe Transport, Pen & Sword Select,
Pen & Sword Military Classics, Leo Cooper, The Praetorian Press,
Remember When, Seaforth Publishing and Frontline Publishing.

For a complete list of Pen & Sword titles please contact
PEN & SWORD BOOKS LIMITED
47 Church Street, Barnsley, South Yorkshire, S70 2AS, England
E-mail: enquiries@pen-and-sword.co.uk
Website: www.pen-and-sword.co.uk

CONTENTS

DICKENS ON WILLS AFFECTION – OR HATRED?

We naturally fell into a train of reflection as we walked homewards, upon the curious old records of likings and dislikings; of jealousies and revenges; of affection defying the power of death, and hatred pursued beyond the grave, which these depositories contain; silent but striking tokens, some of them, of excellence of heart, and nobleness of soul; melancholy examples, others, of the worst passions of human nature. How many men, as they lay speechless and helpless on the bed of death would have given worlds but for the strength and power to blot out the silent animosity and bitterness, which now stands registered against them in Doctors' Commons!

Charles Dickens, *Sketches by Boz*

ACKNOWLEDGEMENTS

I have been contemplating a book on this topic for over twenty years, and I am grateful to my publishers for at long last persuading me to do something about it. Simon Fowler commissioned the book, and has provided much useful input. My thanks are also due to Jeremy Gibson, whose book on Probate jurisdictions proved indispensible for the compilation of my list of probate courts. He read an early draft of my text and provided valuable advice.

I am also indebted to the various owners of copyright who have allowed me to reproduce their illustrations. Their names are noted underneath the illustrations. Crown copyright images are reproduced by courtesy of The National Archives, London, England and findmypast.co.uk.

My primary debt, however, is to the editors of the innumerable editions of published probate records listed below, pp. 110-30, whose work I have drawn on extensively.

INTRODUCTION

The Value of Probate Records

Probate records are invaluable sources of information for family and local historians. Wills in particular enable us to get closer to our ancestors than most other documents. They are usually the only official documents available that were written at the express direction of our ancestors, and may provide a detailed insight into their beliefs, their families, and their material life. Sometimes, our ancestors' personalities shine through. When Sir William Trevanion of St Michael Caerhays (Cornwall) made his will in 1512, the high regard he had for his wife Agnes was made evident in his concern that she should, in due course, share his marble tomb, and have her arms displayed on it, provided that she did not remarry.

Other probate documents are also important, and should not be neglected. Inventories list the goods of the deceased; accounts reveal how those goods have been disposed of; administration bonds identify those charged with administering the estates of intestates; the records of disputes in the probate courts provide us with much information about life as seen by the common man. All of these documents give us valuable insights into the daily lives of our ancestors.

Men have been writing wills in England for over a thousand years. They are still being written today. Millions survive, mostly from the mid-fifteenth century onwards, when ecclesiastical probate courts began registering and storing them. They are accompanied by a variety of related documents, such as probate inventories, administration bonds, and executors' accounts. Much can be learnt from these documents. For the family historian, they provide invaluable evidence for family relationships. The local historian can find in them much of the information required to reconstruct past communities.

Probate records can be found in many different record offices, both local and national, throughout England and Wales. This book will focus primarily on English and Welsh probate records dating from the medieval era to 1857. In that year, the ecclesiastical probate system was abolished, and a completely new structure was created. Some guidance will be given on using post-1857 wills, and on the probate records of other jurisdictions within the British Isles. Most of the examples given are taken from the published collections of probate records listed below, pp. 110–30.

The Survival of Wills

It has been calculated that the number of wills proved in English probate courts rose from an average of under five hundred per annum before 1500, to perhaps 5,000 or 6,000 per annum at the end of the seventeenth century. Not all of these documents survive. The ravages of fire, water, dirt, mice,

The ravages of mice: a damaged account. (Courtesy of Todd Grey)

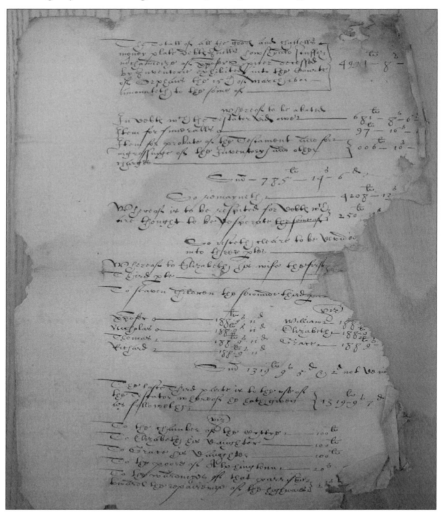

2

and other predators have taken their toll. Many have been lost or destroyed. The canons of 1604 claimed that archdeaconry and peculiar courts had been much more inefficient than the higher courts, as many had 'no known nor certain registrars nor public place to keep their records in'. Act books frequently record the grant of probate for wills which are lost. For example, most Archdeaconry of Cornwall wills for the sixteenth century have disappeared. Grants of probate for the missing wills were recorded in the Archdeaconry's act books, so we know what was once available. Only a handful of pre-1660 inventories for Herefordshire survived the destruction wrought in the diocesan archives during the Civil War. In Durham, testamentary documents were especially favoured for lighting pipes! Many probate records for Devon were destroyed in the Exeter Blitz. Fortunately, many of the destroyed wills had been transcribed before they were destroyed, and others had been indexed. The Devon Wills Project **http://genuki.cs. ncl.ac.uk/DEV/DevonWillsProject** is currently compiling an index to all surviving wills for the county, including copies.

The destruction of Devon wills was exceptional; the only other comparable loss of probate records occurred when the Irish Public Record Office was blown up in 1922. Some wills survive for the great majority of British probate courts, although holdings are not necessarily as complete as they should be. The will registers of the Prerogative Court of Canterbury (PCC) are particularly extensive; no fewer than 1,016,197 wills can be found on Documents Online **www.nationalarchives.gov.uk/documentsonline**, dating from 1384 to 1858. Other probate documents have not fared as well. Inventories for Essex, for example, are scarce. Probate accounts only survive for a small proportion of decedents.

Various different probate systems operated in the British Isles; most of this book deals with the English and Welsh system. The other British jurisdictions – the Channel Islands, Ireland, the Isle of Man, and Scotland – are discussed in Chapter 8.

The Origin of Wills

Originally, wills were spoken in the presence of witnesses, rather than written. The custom of writing them down began in the Anglo-Saxon period. Fewer than 100 wills from this period now survive (edited in Dorothy Whitelock's *Anglo-Saxon wills*, Cambridge University Press, 1930), although there were probably many more. The prime motivation for making these written wills was religious in character. The church encouraged giving to pious causes, preferably during life, but also in the form of bequests. Written wills gave greater security for the fulfilment of such bequests.

Gradually, the church became more interested in ensuring that pious bequests were enforced. That interest was reinforced when William the

Conqueror decided to withdraw 'spiritual' pleas from the secular courts. Pious bequests became subject to ecclesiastical jurisdiction. Over the next two centuries, separate ecclesiastical courts were gradually established. They operated under canon law, which was binding on the clergy, but could be challenged by laymen under common law. The jurisdiction of bishops over pious bequests was gradually extended until they exercised jurisdiction over all bequests of chattels. By the thirteenth century, the church courts were requiring executors to prove testaments before them. Magna Carta (1225) granted supervision of intestate estates to the church, and a statute of 1357 required administrators of intestate estates to apply for grants of administration. Nevertheless, ecclesiastical powers were limited. The only sanctions their courts could impose to ensure the proper administration of estates, and the payment of legacies, were the humiliating imposition of public penance, and the more serious excommunication. Imprisonment or the sentence of death could only be imposed by lay courts.

There was another important limitation on the powers of both testators and ecclesiastics. The medieval Crown's claims as feudal overlord prevented bequests of landed property (realty), except in the case of some burgage tenures. Jurisdiction over the descent of land remained with the secular courts, even though the latter came to recognize the ecclesiastically-approved executor as the deceased's personal representative. Ecclesiastics only had jurisdiction over moveable goods, not over realty. Strictly speaking, they could only prove the testament, which bequeathed moveable goods. With a few exceptions, wills devising realty could not be made before the law was changed in the early sixteenth century.

The Statute of Wills of 1540, for the first time, allowed realty to be devised by will. Once this legislation was passed, the will and testament were usually merged in one document. The term 'will' came to be used as short-hand for the joint 'will and testament', although ecclesiastical jurisdiction was still limited to moveable property. Matters relating to the inheritance of real property continued to be subject to the jurisdiction of equity and common law courts.

The church was well-placed to supervise the processes of will-making and probate. In medieval Lincoln Diocese, Canon Foster has described the parish priest as 'the first and principal witness' of most wills. The making of the will was regarded as part of preparation for death. Assistance in that process was a major function of the priest. It was the pastoral duty of the clergy to visit when their parishioners were sick and dying. In the medieval period, they were sometimes the only local people able to write. It was natural to call upon them to act as scribes of wills, and then to ensure that bequests were properly carried out.

The growth of literacy following the Reformation meant that the clergy had to share their duties as scribes with others. There were an increasing number of people able to act as scribes. In Reading (Berkshire), there were eleven professional scrivenors active between 1660 and 1699. However, the *Book of Common Prayer*, which even today is still in use in some Anglican parishes, continued to expect that the clergy should admonish the sick to make their wills. The rubric required clergy to frequently put men 'in remembrance to take order for the settling of their temporal estates, whilst they are in health'.

Ecclesiastical jurisdiction over probate in England and Wales remained in force until January 1858, when it was transferred to the secular Court of Probate. Most wills proved before then must be sought amongst ecclesiastical archives. In other jurisdictions, the date at which secular courts took over probate varied. The Scottish Commissary Courts were secular from 1560, but the Ecclesiastical Court of the Bailiwick of Guernsey exercises ecclesiastical probate jurisdiction to this day.

The English secular courts have, however, always exercised jurisdiction over some matters related to probate. Landed property descended by primogeniture, or by manorial custom, and was subject to equity courts such as Chancery. It could be devised by will, but not bequeathed by testament. By the sixteenth century, wills and testaments had been merged in England and Wales, but the legal distinction remained. Similarly, debts owed to and by testators were matters for the common law. Executors and administrators could sue and be sued for debt in King's Bench and other common law courts.

Probate Law

The law affecting probate was complex, and occupied much space in legal text books of the seventeenth and eighteenth centuries. Surviving probate records reflect this reality. They were written for legal purposes, not for historians. They aimed to comply with the requirements of the law. The law did not require the comprehensiveness that historians would like, and probate records do not always include the information that would give a fully rounded picture of a decedent's wealth or the descent of property. The standard format used by both wills and inventories hides the fact that some matters could not be subjected to probate in the ecclesiastical courts. These documents are not necessarily as comprehensive as they may seem.

Legally, a valid will required three elements. It had to be dated, to name an executor and to be signed by the testator in the presence of witnesses. In 1529, a number of statutory obligations were laid on testators. They were expected to ensure that their debts were paid, that their wives and children were provided for, and that some charitable provisions were made from their estate. The study of probate records is, at least in part, the study of how these provisions were carried out.

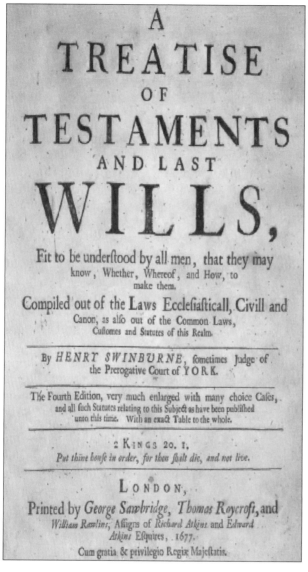

A TREATISE

OF

TESTAMENTS AND LAST

WILLS,

Fit to be underftood by all men, that they may know, Whether, Whereof, and How, to make them.

Compiled out of the Laws Ecclefiaticall, Civill and Canon, as alfo out of the Common Laws, Cuftomes and Statutes of this Realm.

By *HENRY SWINBURNE*, fometimes Judge of the Prerogative Court of YORK.

The Fourth Edition, very much enlarged with many choice Cafes, and all fuch Statutes relating to this Subject as have been publifhed unto this time. With an exact Table to the whole.

2 KINGS 20. 1.

Put thine houfe in order, for thou fhalt die, and not live.

LONDON,

Printed by *George Sawbridge, Thomas Roycroft,* and *William Rawlins;* Affigns of *Richard Atkins* and *Edward Atkins* Efquires, 1677.

Cum gratia & privilegio Regis Majeftatis.

Swinburne's Treatise of Testaments – *a leading textbook for sixteenth and seventeenth-century lawyers. This is the fourth edition.*

Probate records are generally well indexed and accessible. Many indexes are readily available on the internet. It is also possible to actually read many wills online. Reference has already been made to TNA's Documents Online database of PCC wills **www.nationalarchives.gov.uk/documentsonline**. A number of similar collections are currently available, and others are currently being digitized. These developments make it possible to undertake research which would have been impossible a few years ago.

A huge amount of information is available in probate records. They mention many names – not only testators and legatees, but also scribes, executors, administrators, witnesses, appraisers, court officials, and others. They also mention many relationships. The terms used for relationships are not necessarily those used today. A kinsman was simply a relation. A son-in-law could be a step-son. Cousins could be nieces or nephews. The 1653 will of John Cater of Kings Langley (Hertfordshire) spells it out: he bequeathed £20 to 'my cozen Elizabeth Cater, daughter of my brother Robert Cater'.

The most important relationships, then as now, were spouses and children. Wills are almost certain to name widows and surviving children, thus providing basic genealogical information. If you can trace a run of family wills, you may be able to construct a pedigree without consulting any other source.

The value of wills goes beyond the construction of pedigrees. They may tell you where your ancestor lived, who lived with him, who his friends were, his religious opinions, his occupation and/or status, how he sought to provide for his children, and a whole host of other personal details. They are the most personal documents concerning ancestors – especially ancestors of three or four centuries ago – that most family historians are likely to discover. They provide snapshots of your ancestors' personal worlds in a way that no other documents can. They comprise the only major series of official records that were compiled at the direction of ancestors, rather than at the direction of bureaucrats.

Probate inventories also provide much useful information. They reveal the wealth of our ancestors, and the material conditions in which they lived. They provide another snapshot of ancestors' lives, enabling you to picture them in their houses using fireside implements and kitchen utensils to prepare their food, whilst a side of bacon 'hung at the roof' above them. They describe the furniture in the house, and may list the rooms in which beds, tableboards, chairs, and other furniture were used. They take you outside and list the animals in the yard, the crops in the fields, and the implements farmers used.

Significant events could also be recorded. The sufferings of Robert and Jane Thompson of Ryhope (Co. Durham) during the Civil War are described in graphic detail in their probate account, written in 1646. It includes a detailed listing of 'such goods and chattels of the said deceased as were violently taken from him by the severall armies then resideing in the county for their present reliefe and supply, being quartered upon them, as also such necessary summes and disbursements as were payd ... in asseessments and billettinge'. The total loss amounted to £335 10s 4d. The consequences of disaster for our ancestors could be serious: the Thompsons had no insurance.

Probate records enable you to appreciate what it was like to live before the industrial revolution, in an era when most people depended on the local harvest, produced their own food, made their own clothes and household goods, and did not know what mass production was. The study of these documents gives us an insight into how our ancestors lived.

The local historian can study a huge range of topics using probate records. Religion, occupations, inheritance, migration, literacy, agriculture, housing, furniture, industry and trade, wealth, charitable giving, vernacular architecture, can all be – and have been – subjected to detailed investigation by using wills and inventories. Accounts may be used to study funeral customs and the credit market, amongst other topics. Even the humble administration bond may provide useful information on relationships, or on the experience of orphans and the role of guardians.

If all the probate documents for particular individuals are studied together, and compared with other evidence, such as parish registers, tax lists, and deeds, much can be learnt about the history of both particular families, and entire communities. Some students have used thousands of wills and inventories as a basis for their research. The problems of handling large quantities of data, and of using statistical sampling, have been discussed at length by Weatherill, in her *Consumer behaviour and material culture in Britain 1660–1760* (2nd ed. Routledge, 1996) and, more mathematically, by Overton et al in *Production and consumption in English households, 1600–1750.* (Routledge, 2004).

Some Limitations and Biases

The possibilities should not blind the researcher to the pitfalls. Probate records contain a huge amount of detail, but not all probate records are equally reliable. Some provide exceptionally detailed information about a wide range of topics; others are terse in the extreme.

Before these documents can be analysed their limitations must be pointed out. Their representativeness, trustworthiness, and completeness must all be examined. To start with, the language and idiosyncratic nature of probate records can be problematic. Many objects mentioned in them have ceased to be common household goods, and many of the words used to describe them are obsolescent. There are no longer cranes in hearths, or pewter dishes on tableboards. Trestles for the latter are rarely used in people's houses. The chaffing dish (used for keeping food hot) and the posnet (a small cooking pot which stood over the open fire) have quite disappeared from daily life.

The idiosyncratic way in which probate records were written also makes analysis difficult. Their scribes could be inquisitive or bored, laconic or careful, unobservant or keen to display their descriptive powers. Arithmetic was not always appraisers' strong point. Some inventories can be brief to the point of terseness, for example, simply listing 'wearing apparell', or 'all other lumber'. Others can provide very detailed descriptions. What one describes as a chair can, for another, be 'an elboe chair with red turkey work on it'. The prolixity of one appraiser can illumine the taciturnity of others. Comparisons of the language used in various different inventories can provide much deeper understanding of their meanings overall.

There are a variety of reasons why an inventory may be an incomplete record of an individual's possessions. A basic understanding of probate law is necessary to understand some of the deliberate exclusions. For example, freehold land is frequently not mentioned, as it was outside of the juris-diction of ecclesiastical probate courts. Inventories were not required to record debts owed by the deceased (although this difficulty can be remedied if accounts are available). A variety of other legal requirements governed the recording of items such as food, crops, and animals. Apart from these legal issues, goods may have been disposed of by the deceased before death, or removed by legatees before the inventory was compiled. Seasonality may have an impact on the values of livestock and arable crops.

There are also a variety of biases in any collection of probate records from a particular place. They are only available for those who had reason to make a will (discussed in Chapter 1), or whose heirs thought it necessary to obtain a grant of administration. Such people were generally the wealthier members of a community, so there is a bias against the poor. The Clee (Lincolnshire) burial register lists eighty-five labourers buried between 1609 and 1640. There are only inventories for seven. By contrast, six yeomen were buried; there are inventories for all but one of them. A part of the reason for this bias is, of course, the fact that the law did not require estates valued at under £5 to pass through the probate process. Further, there were no fees to be had by proving the wills of poor testators.

There is also, obviously, an age bias. Wills were made at the end of life, and could not be made by minors. They ignore the life cycle, and the fact that wealth varied with age. Most inventories list goods accumulated over many years; we have few inventories for young servants.

Wills are also biased against women, since wives could only make them with the consent of their husbands. The majority of wills for females relate to widows.

Reconstructing Historical Communities: a Case Study

Despite these limitations, probate records constitute a valuable resource for reconstructing historical communities, and numerous local studies have been based upon them. The possibilities open to local historians will be illustrated here by using Week St Mary (Cornwall) as a case study.

One of the keys to understanding the history of any community is the religion it professes. Wills provide useful evidence for testators' religious beliefs. Most commence with a religious preamble and an expression of faith. The evidence of these preambles has been used extensively to determine the progress of the Reformation in the sixteenth century. The lack of sixteenth-century probate records prevents this type of investigation in Week St Mary. However, in the following century the changing phraseology of religious clauses can be used to demonstrate a growing awareness of religious doctrine.

Expressions of faith usually include bequests of the soul. These may be divided into two categories: the formal bequest of the soul to 'almighty God my maker and redeemer', or its equivalent, and bequests which express deeply-felt beliefs. The latter may perhaps be described as 'proclamatory bequests': they proclaim the saving work of Christ, the forgiveness of sins, the assurance of salvation, and the expectation of everlasting life in the Kingdom of God. Such bequests are much more likely to reflect the beliefs of the testator (or perhaps of the scribe) than more formal phraseology. In Week St Mary, only eight per cent of wills in the first quarter of the seventeenth century made proclamatory bequests. In the final quarter of the century, the figure was fifty-five per cent. These figures suggest that, even allowing for the influence of scribes and the use of will formularies, knowledge of the Bible was much more widespread in this remote parish at the end of the century than it was at the beginning.

The geographical horizons of local people provide another key to understanding historical communities. Many places are mentioned in probate records – not just the abode of the decedent, but also the abodes of legatees, debtors, and others involved in the process of probate, the places where decedents owned lands, and the places executors had to visit in order to prove wills. All of this is valuable information for tracing the area with which local people were familiar, and is worth combining with similar information from other sources, such as parish registers. For Week St Mary, this evidence enables us to conclude that the horizons of most local people were very limited, and that most rarely travelled outside of a radius of about ten miles from the parish. Even local market towns such as Holsworthy (Devon) and Camelford (Cornwall) were rarely visited, much less regional centres such as Exeter and Plymouth. Very few Week St Mary inhabitants ever saw London – although in the fifteenth century one became Lady Mayoress (and subsequently a great benefactress to her home parish), and in the sixteenth century another rode to the capital under duress, and nearly lost his head for his participation in the 1549 prayer book rebellion! Only the gentry and the local clergy were used to travel. Most rectors had studied at Oxford, and the leading gentle family – the Rolles – were a junior branch of the major land-owning family in Devon, whose estate they eventually inherited.

Probate records throw much light on occupations, either by directly stating the occupations of decedents, or by recording equipment such as anvils (for blacksmiths) or vats (for dyers). This information enables us to examine the economic life of the community. In Week St Mary, many decedents were husbandmen (smallholders, who perhaps rented thirty acres) and yeomen (more substantial tenant farmers). The term 'farmer' was not used in its present sense in the seventeenth century.

In addition to the agriculturalists, the probate records mention many weavers and spinners, with their looms and 'turns' (spinning wheels). A number of other rural crafts are also mentioned – blacksmiths, carpenters, coopers. There is one will for a miller, and two probate inventories. Another miller – a member of the Clifton family – can be identified because he is mentioned in the will of another testator.

No apprentices are mentioned in extant Week St Mary documentation, but probate records frequently mention them elsewhere. Testators commonly sought to provide for their children by bequeathing a sum to pay for apprenticeship premiums, which may also be recorded in probate accounts.

Another type of evidence for occupations is provided by handwriting. Cornelius Clifton's hand can be clearly seen on fourteen different probate documents, including both wills and inventories, written for parishioners. Evidence in other sources indicates that he came from a family of minor attorneys. Acting as a scribe was clearly one way in which he earned his living. Most other parishes had similar semi-professionals.

In other places, it may be possible to single out particular occupations, such as blacksmiths or weavers, for detailed study. Amongst the archives of the Archdeaconry of Cornwall, for example, there are sixty-nine tinners' wills. In Worcester, Alan Dyer (*The city of Worcester in the sixteenth century*, Leicester University Press, 1973) has shown from wills that fifty-four per cent of tradesmen between 1590 and 1620 were engaged in the cloth trade.

Occupational labels in the early modern period can only take us so far. They tend to hide the fact that many people had more than one occupation. Ralph Hartland's Week St Mary inventory of 1663/4 listed 'merchantry ware', together with an old nag and packsaddles for carrying his goods: he was probably a chapman. He may also have worked as a tinker, and he had combs for combing wool.

The inventories from Week St Mary make it clear that, whatever the occupational designations given to decedents, the great majority of the population were involved in husbandry. Over seventy-five per cent of inventories mention either livestock or arable crops. Even where there is no such mention, it is highly likely that the decedents concerned were nevertheless dependent on the land; they included two gentlemen, four yeomen, four husbandmen, and two labourers.

The inventories reveal an overwhelming emphasis on animal husbandry, and especially on cattle, in seventeenth-century Week St Mary. Livestock accounted for some eighty per cent of the total value of agricultural commodities. However, cattle herds were usually small, averaging perhaps only eight or ten beasts. Many sheep and pigs were also kept.

Farmers and their families supplied most of the labour force on agricultural holdings. Servants are rarely mentioned, except in the wills of leading parishioners. Most holdings were small, and had no need of them.

The most prosperous occupations can be identified by comparing occupational information with the total values of chattels shown on inventories. There are of course dangers in doing this – inventories alone do not reveal debts owed by decedents, nor do they record the ownership of freehold property. They do, however, provide evidence of the flow of wealth. In Week St Mary, they show that the wealthiest inhabitants were the yeomen, who leased substantial holdings. Some fourteen per cent of seventeenth-century inventories valued at under £10 record leases of land. The comparable figure for inventories valued at over £100 is sixty-two per cent.

It is also possible to use wealth totals from inventories to compare the prosperity of the community as a whole with that of other communities. This comparison demonstrates that Week St Mary was perhaps the poorest parish whose inventories have been studied in detail. Paradoxically, that explains why there were probably few paupers. As Cobbett noted two centuries later, a rich land was apt to breed poor labourers, but a poor or wooded countryside promised them prosperity.

The wealth totals of inventories can also be used to demonstrate increasing material prosperity, especially in the final decade of the seventeenth century. In the first decade of the century, the mean value of inventories was just over £36; in the final decade the figure was just over £65.

This growth was reflected in the goods that people owned. At the beginning of the century, household possessions were sparse. By the end of the century, that could no longer be said, although the inhabitants of Week St Mary were still poor in relationship to most other parishes. Our study of the parish ends in 1700. It is clear, however, that wealth continued to accumulate, and that household goods continued to proliferate. Their sheer number was probably one of the factors which led to the demise of the probate inventory. It was simply not worth the time and effort of the appraisers to list everything.

Inventories provide us with a huge amount of detail concerning material life, and how people lived. In many places, they enumerate the contents of a house room by room, and thus provide a detailed picture of the house itself. Thirty of the seventy-three inventories for Sunderland (Co. Durham) record rooms in decedents' houses. The uses to which rooms were put reflect cultural assumptions, aspirations, and changing social norms. At the end of the medieval period, the hall was the hub of the household's life, and the only heated room. It has now become merely the entrance to the house. Similarly, beds have been removed from downstairs parlours to upstairs bedrooms. Changes such as these can be traced through the study of probate inventories.

Sadly, there are no room by room listings amongst Week St Mary inventories. The parish was poor, and the hearth tax of 1662–4 reveals that seventy-five per cent of houses only had one or two hearths. Most appraisers had to list goods in only one or two rooms, and did not bother to itemise them separately. The most detailed description of a Week St Mary house in the probate records is in fact in a will, rather than an inventory. George Leigh's house at Groves End had an entry, a hall, a parlour, and a chamber over the parlour. There was also a separate cellar with a chamber over, and a separate bakehouse. This was a comfortable house by Week St Mary standards; Leigh was a member of one of the parish's leading families.

Even when inventories do record the rooms in a house, it cannot be assumed that they provide complete descriptions. There was no obligation on appraisers to include rooms which were empty. Rooms occupied by lodgers, or perhaps by other family members, would not have been recorded.

The interiors of seventeenth-century houses were bare by modern standards. Week St Mary houses were places to work, eat, and sleep in; they were not designed for leisure or relaxation. Inventories demonstrate that working space dominated living space.

Increasing wealth led to a revolution in attitudes towards wealth, and towards material comfort. That revolution can be traced by studying the furniture, the kitchen utensils, and the fireside equipment, in probate inventories. For example, in 1577 William Harrison (in his *The description of England* www.fordham.edu/halsall/mod/1577harrison-england.asp) noted that, in the recent past, most people had slept 'upon straw pallets, on rough mats covered only with a sheet, under coverlets made of dagswain or hapharlots ... and a good round log under their heads'. The transformation in material comfort that he recorded is reflected in Week St Mary, where, in 1600, even the poorest decedents in Week St Mary had beds. They were usually the most valuable items of furniture in a house, and perhaps a status symbol.

Other items of furniture were not found quite so frequently. At the beginning of the seventeenth century, many Week St Mary houses had no tables, and even fewer had chairs. Numbers increased substantially during the century. Apart from furniture, inventories record many utensils and other household items. These, too, were subject to change. Pewter, for example, is recorded in forty-five per cent of inventories between 1600 and 1624, and eighty-three per cent between 1675 and 1699. The value of fireside equipment such as andirons, spits, and pot-hangings also increased towards the end of the seventeenth century, as items became more numerous and elaborate. The post-1700 inventories for Week St Mary have not been studied, but it is likely that table knives and forks, not mentioned at all before 1700, became usual by the mid-eighteenth century. Nevertheless, Week St Mary remained comparatively poor. It did not have the musical instruments, the billiard tables, or the playing cards, which were beginning to appear in inventories from Cornish towns from around 1700. Nor did it have the wall hangings and pictures which covered many walls in cathedral cities such as Lichfield. And books were rarely mentioned.

The absence of books did not mean that parishioners were illiterate. There is little direct evidence for schools and schoolmasters in Week St Mary, but local people must have been taught to write, since their writing skills are evident in every probate document. These provide good evidence for the extent of literacy in the parish. Close scrutiny of the handwriting in them reveals that there were at least 145 people in the parish capable of writing probate documents in the course of the seventeenth century.

Autographs provide more information. Testators, appraisers, witnesses, and others, all had to sign their names, and thus revealed whether they were literate. The extent of literacy can be suggested by counting the respective numbers of signatures and marks. This is, admittedly, a rough and ready method of investigation, especially bearing in mind the fact that the ability to read did not imply the ability to write. Nevertheless, counting does give us some idea of how many people could write. It reveals that there was much fluctuation in the extent of literacy throughout the century. In the 1690s, however, the proportion of signatures was much higher than had been usual in previous decades. This was associated with the fact that women began signing their own names in the 1690s. In the previous ninety years, only one had ever done so. The probate documents clearly establish that literacy was increasing at the end of the seventeenth century. It is likely that educational provision in Week St Mary was also beginning to increase at the end of the seventeenth century.

Some other Topics for Study

There are many other ways in which probate records can be studied. The dissemination of new goods, such as beds in the sixteenth century, pewter in the seventeenth century, and tea cups in the eighteenth century, can be traced using inventories. So can the introduction of new crops, such as turnips, clover, and potatoes. Attitudes to death and dying can be traced not only through the provisions of wills, but also through the expenditure incurred by executors on funerals. Much of what we know about the credit market in Tudor and Stuart England is based on the lists of 'sperate' and 'desperate' debts in inventories. It is even possible to study the increasing use of arabic numerals in different places by counting the number of inventories which use them in preference to Roman numerals. Anyone interested in the family, religious, and material lives of our ancestors will find a huge amount of information by studying the probate records they left behind.

The following chapters explore these issues in greater detail, considering questions such as why wills were made, what can be found in them and other probate documents, how they can be located, and how they can be used.

Chapter 1

WHO MADE WILLS? AND WHY DID THEY MAKE THEM?

Although wills are common documents, not everyone made one. Perhaps half the population were legally incapable of writing a valid will. Married women could only make a will with the express consent of their husbands. Until 1882, they could not hold property in their own right. Minors, that is boys under fourteen and girls under twelve, could not make a will at all. According to Richard Burn's *New law dictionary*, published in 1792:

> madmen, idiots, or natural fools, persons grown childish by age or infirmity, and such as have their senses besotted with drunkenness, so persons born deaf and dumb, persons under fear or restraint, or circumvented by fraud, persons outlawed, excommunicate, attainted of treason or felony, are incapable to make a will, so long as such disability may last.

Many wills make the point that the testator was 'of sound and perfect memory': those who were not, could not make them.

Wills could generally be written by adult males, and by widowed or unmarried females. Even so, not everyone entitled to make one did so. Not everyone needed one. The poor had no need of a will: they had nothing to bequeath (although some wills do survive even for the poorest). A widower with only one son had no need to make a will if he intended everything to go to his heir. For most people, the purpose of a will was to make provision for their spouses, and for any children who had not already been established on a farm or in some trade. In Powick (Worcestershire), only 11.9 per cent of bequests were made to people who were not members of the testator's family.

A number of studies have investigated how many people made wills. Proportions vary across the country, ranging from as low as eight per cent in Earls Colne (Essex) in the late sixteenth century, to perhaps a third in Elizabethan Kent, to almost a half in early seventeenth-century Banbury (Oxfordshire). Banbury was a peculiar (see glossary, p. 173), and its church-wardens may have had some interest in the fees due to the peculiar court.

They frequently presented executors at ecclesiastical visitations if they did not apply for a grant of probate. Their presentments ensured that a substantial number of wills were proved. They were not alone. In 1741, visitation articles directed to the clergy of the Diocese of Canterbury asked the question, 'are any wills or testaments of persons deceased, within your parish that you know of, yet unprov'd? Or any goods administred without a due Grant from the Ordinary?' Similar inquiries in the Diocese of Salisbury may help to explain the substantial number of diocesan wills now held by Wiltshire and Swindon History Centre.

It is not clear whether visitation articles in other dioceses placed the same requirement on churchwardens. Probably, most churchwardens were not as zealous as those in Banbury. The Registrar General calculated that, in England and Wales, only one person in ten left a will in 1858, the first year of the new Court of Probate. For adult males, the proportion rose to 15.2 per cent. The majority of people did not leave wills. Many had no motive to do so.

By the fifteenth century, the original religious motive for making a will had become little more than a pious hope in the thoughts of clergymen. In 1540 the Statute of Wills gave testators authority to devise realty by will. From this date, the value of a will was that it gave testators the ability to control the disposition of their entire estates. In Scotland, the law denied testators an unrestricted right to dispose of their property. Consequently, fewer wills were made. In England and Wales, testators were relatively free to make decisions, except in the Province of York. There, customary law prevailed until 1692: one-third of an estate had to be given to the widow, and one-third to children, leaving only the remaining third available for testators to distribute.

Despite the relative freedom of testators in the Province of Canterbury, many were happy to allow custom and the law of primogeniture to take its course, and either made no will, or did not mention their real estate in their wills. Nevertheless, gentlemen and yeomen were far more likely to make wills than labourers; they had property to bequeath.

Amongst the gentry, it was common for land to be settled. Settled land was legally owned by trustees; heads of families held it for their own life only. Such life interests could not be devised by will. If, however, the family estate was not already settled, the will itself might be used as a means of settling the estate on the heirs for two or perhaps three generations. The gentry and nobility increasingly sought to preserve their family estates by restricting the ability of descendants to dispose of them.

The primary concern of testators was to provide for young children and/or widows, to settle complicated personal affairs, to ensure that the undeserving did not inherit, and – sometimes – to make charitable bequests,

17

if only to compensate the church for 'tithes forgot'. If reasons such as these did not exist, it was not necessary to make a will.

In the *Merry Wives of Windsor*, Shakespeare expresses the popular attitude to will-making when he makes Slender say 'I ne'er made my will yet, I thank heaven. I am not such a sickly creature, I give heaven praise'. Making a will whilst you were fit and healthy might tempt fate, and accelerate death. Most adopted this approach, despite the injunctions of the *Book of Common Prayer*. William Assheton's *Theological discourse of last wills and testaments*, published in 1696, urged readers to 'make your will in the time of your health. And do not defer so weighty a work, which requires both leisure and composedness of mind, to your death-bed'. Few followed his advice.

The process of will-making frequently began with the summons of neighbours to attend at a death-bed. Once the will had been made, the testator promptly died. In Darlington (Co. Durham), Thomas Catherick lived for 155 days after making his will in 1608. Most testators died much sooner than this, and none in Darlington survived any longer. In 1479, William Ive of St Albans (Hertfordshire) referred to the 'futility of recording my testament in writing'. He was probably suffering from the plague, and meant that the scribe would not have time to write his will before he died. Despite appearances to the contrary, however, making a will could be a lengthy process, and might require several drafts. The records of probate litigation frequently recount the process of will-making. They demonstrate that, sometimes, wills were prepared long before death, but only dated and signed when death was imminent. One testator in North Devon had already made a will, but 'he wolde have a newe Wyll made accordnge to the old wyll worde by worde Even as the other wylle was because he wold sett all thyngs at Ryght'. He 'wolde have yt newe dated & new Wytnes because the old weare ded'. One wonders if premonitions of death amongst sixteenth and seventeenth-century testators were always as accurate as wills make them appear to have been.

There were occasions meriting the making of a will whilst the testator was still healthy. The seamen of the Cleveland area (Yorkshire) were engaged in a hazardous occupation; their wills were sometimes made many years before their deaths. Departure on a long and hazardous journey, an inheritance, a serious illness, marriage, or the birth of children, might all prompt action. Deryk Leke's will of 1546 begins with the statement that 'I ... most nedes taky my viage beyonde the sea to my frendys'. He paid tax as an alien, and was probably going to visit his continental relatives. Whether he came back is not clear, but his will is transcribed in the will register of the Consistory Court of London. Adrian Barthelmey of London made his will whilst he was actually on a journey; he was 'intending to travel towards London' when he was forced to halt at St Albans 'because of plague' in 1479. His will was proved in St Albans.

A rather different reason lay behind William Catesby's 1485 will. He may have been in good health – but he was also under sentence of death for his participation in the Battle of Bosworth. In his will, he made his feelings concerning some of his fellows quite clear: 'My Lordis Stanley, Strange, and all that blood, help and pray for my soule for ye have not for my body as I trusted in you'.

Wills were written on paper or parchment. The testator sometimes wrote the will himself. Such wills are known as holographs. Wills written on printed forms can also sometimes be found. More frequently, a scribe was required. Medieval wills are likely to be in Latin. English tended to be used from the sixteenth century onwards. Sometimes, Latin wills were interspersed with English, showing where scribes could not think of the appropriate Latin word. The will of Edward Atwell of Northampton (1485) goes further; its scribe began to write in Latin but, faced with the need to translate numerous different terms, gave up, and wrote the rest of the document in English. Many of the St Albans (Hertfordshire) wills for 1471–1500 may have been translated from the English of the original wills into Latin when they were copied into the register. In the medieval period, the scribe was usually a clergyman, since he was the only member of the community who was literate.

Clergymen continued to write and witness wills throughout the period 1500–1800. In South Elmham (Suffolk), thirty-four per cent of wills in the period 1550 to 1640 were either witnessed by clergymen, or named them as executors. In Sunderland (Co. Durham), two-thirds of wills written between 1551 and 1575 were witnessed by clergymen; the proportion dropped to less than a sixth between 1626 and 1650. The clergy ceased to be the only scribes. The rise in lay literacy enabled testators to choose their scribe, rather than being forced to rely on the only literate person in the parish – the incumbent. Sometimes, the unpopularity of the ecclesiastical establishment encouraged them to seek out lay help. George Lilburn of Sunderland (Co. Durham) was notorious for his opposition to the Durham diocesan establishment; he appeared as a witness (and probably as a scribe) to wills more frequently than most local clergy.

Surviving wills reveal the hands of many village attorneys who had a smattering of training in the law. Frauncis Genyver, a mere labourer of Grimsbury (Northamptonshire), paid no less than 2s 6d to the writer of his will in 1600. His inventory totalled a mere £12 1s. In the remote Cornish parish of Week St Mary, no fewer than five semi-professional scribes have been identified in the seventeenth century. The clergy in this parish were not asked to write wills. Wills provide valuable evidence for the activities of attorneys at grass-roots level. They were not, however, alone. The substantial number of Week St Mary laymen who wrote wills has already been pointed out: there was a surprising degree of literacy in this remote Cornish parish.

The scribe would attend the death bed in order to ascertain the wishes of the testator, then go away and write the will. Many used published will formularies to help them with the wording, although these were not necessarily copied slavishly. When he had completed his text, the scribe would return and read it to the testator in the presence of witnesses. If the testator approved, both he and the witnesses would sign it (or make their mark). This would provide legal confirmation that the testator was of 'sound mind', and thus legally capable of making his will. The will would then be sealed with hot wax. This was particularly important if the will included devises of real property. Such wills were, in effect, deeds, which had to be sealed to be legally acceptable. Once this had been done, most testators whose wills were subsequently proved died within a few days. Occasionally, the scribe was unable to complete his task before the testator died. If that happened, the will (known as a nuncupative will) might have to be taken to court to be proved in solemn form, by the deposition of witnesses. Such depositions provide much interesting information on the process of will-making.

Chapter 2

WHAT HAPPENED AFTER DEATH? THE PROCESS OF PROBATE

As soon as a testator died, it was incumbent on his or her executor to obtain a grant of probate from a court. Probate is the official recognition of the validity of a will, only granted when the probate court is satisfied that it has been properly witnessed, has not been tampered with, and conforms to other legal requirements. Without probate, executors could not legally act.

If there was no will, the estate of the deceased still had to be administered. The relatives of those who died intestate – without leaving a will – could obtain letters of administration. However, many estates did not pass through the process of probate. It was not thought to be necessary if the value of the estate was small, and there was unlikely to be any dispute about its distribution. A grant was more likely to be applied for if it was necessary to establish a clear legal title to a lease, or if administrators were thought likely to encounter problems. Occasionally, letters of administration were applied for many years after the decedent's death. This could happen if the heir did not bother to apply, but subsequently needed proof of ownership of property – which could be provided by formal letters. Sometimes it was the heir's executor who applied.

Probate Courts

The great majority of probate courts were ecclesiastical courts, although a small number of manorial lords also exercised probate jurisdiction. These courts granted probate, appointed administrators, and judged any disputes that arose within their jurisdictions. The ecclesiastical courts were governed by canon law, but also had to take into account many Parliamentary statutes related to probate (some of the latter are listed in Appendix 5). It is important to understand how probate courts operated.

Since the Norman Conquest, the church has operated at five distinct levels: the parish, the rural deanery, the archdeaconry, the diocese, and the

The dioceses of England from the sixteenth to the nineteenth century.

province. At the base was the parish, cared for by a parish priest. Parishes were grouped together in rural deaneries for administrative purposes. An archdeaconry consisted of several rural deaneries under an archdeacon. Overall control of ecclesiastical administration was in the hands of bishops, whose dioceses were grouped into provinces headed by the two archbishops of Canterbury and York.

Ecclesiastical courts usually operated in archdeaconries, dioceses, and provinces. Prior to 1857, there were hundreds of different probate courts in England and Wales (they are listed in Appendix 1). The majority of wills were proved in archdeaconry courts. Legally, a will should have been proved in the lowest court covering the area in which the testator had goods – not the court covering the area where he lived. A testator whose property was solely in one archdeaconry would normally have his will proved in its court. If he had *bona notabilia* – notable property – in more than one archdeaconry, his executor would go to a diocesan court, normally called the Consistory Court. The Consistory also had the right to hear appeals from archdeaconry courts. Testators who had *bona notabilia* in more than one diocese would have their wills proved in the Prerogative Court of either Canterbury (PCC) or York (PCY) – Canterbury if the *bona notabilia* was in both provinces. The term *bona notabilia* was ill-defined, but generally meant goods valued at more than £5 (or £10 in London). The Prerogative Court could only act if the value of an estate exceeded £5. The wills of those who died overseas, including soldiers and sailors, were proved in the PCC, although, after 1817, the value of their estates had to exceed £20 before the Court could act.

PCC acted as a court of appeal from the diocesan courts. Appeals from PCC lay to either the Court of Arches, or to the High Court of Delegates. The latter took over the functions of the Papal court in Rome from 1533.

There was a tendency for executors to use the more prestigious diocesan and prerogative courts, rather than the lower archdeaconry courts. These courts were not just for the rich and wealthy; 2,603 wills of labourers can be found in PCC. Nonconformists, and especially Quakers, who sought to avoid the attention of local officers, frequently proved their wills in London. After 1810, the Bank of England would only accept wills proved in the PCC as proof of heir's entitlement to inherit government stock. The chances of finding a will in PCC were greatly increased in the early nineteenth century. Many of the smaller courts became moribund before their abolition. In its final decade, PCC proved some forty per cent of wills in England and Wales.

Conversely, not every administrator who ought to have applied for probate to PCC actually did so. In 1490, John Leycester of Northampton bequeathed property in Leicestershire to his wife, but his will was proved in the Archdeaconry Court of Northampton. Similarly, the inventory of Frances Baxter of Little Wenlock (Shropshire), the widow of a minister, is amongst the Hereford Diocesan archives. It shows that some of her goods were located at Haughton, in the parish of Shifnal, which lay in Lichfield Diocese. PCC clearly had jurisdiction, but the Hereford court ignored the fact.

Courts were not normally presided over by the bishops and archdeacons in whose name they sat. They appointed officials (who were variously named) to conduct their business, although they might retain the right to hear cases if they wished. Officials were usually assisted by a registrar, responsible for drawing up court documents such as act books and will registers. Apparitors may also be mentioned in the records. They acted as the court's messengers, executing court mandates, and summoning executors, administrators and witnesses to appear. They seem to have had responsibility for pursuing executors who failed to apply for probate. At the beginning of James I's reign, an apparitor of the Norwich Consistory Court provoked a bitter complaint by citing executors to prove a will even before the testator was buried!

This is a very simplistic outline. The structure of courts varied across the country. The Diocese of Lincoln, for example, had six separate archdeaconries. By contrast, the Diocese of Ely had only one. In some dioceses, bishops had placed probate jurisdiction in the hands of Commissaries, rather than archdeacons. In Leicestershire, the Bishop of Lincoln's Commissary exercised probate jurisdiction over the Archdeaconry of Leicester. In County Durham, matters went even further: the bishops' Consistory Court exercised direct jurisdiction over probate in the archdeaconries. There were no archidiaconal probate courts. In some dioceses, courts were peripatetic. In Lichfield Diocese, for example, whilst the main probate court at Lichfield was in permanent session, other courts travelled on a bi-annual circuit taking in Derby, Chesterfield, Shrewsbury, Newport, Coventry, Coleshill, and Caverswall. Prior to the Civil War, the grants made by these courts were all recorded centrally, although after 1660 they were recorded in separate books for each county in the diocese. The court of the Archdeaconry of Berkshire was similarly peripatetic. It usually sat in Oxford, but sometimes held sessions in Reading, Abingdon, Newbury, and Wallingford.

There were also many 'peculiars', that is, areas outside of the normal jurisdiction of bishops or archdeacons. These were under the jurisdiction of a range of different dignitaries. Buckden (Huntingdonshire) was outside the jurisdiction of the Archdeacon of Huntingdon because it was a peculiar of the Bishop of Lincoln. The abbot of Ely had granted the manor of Buckden to the Bishop in the reign of Henry I; with it went jurisdiction over probate. Temple Newsam (Yorkshire), as its name suggests, had originally been held by successive religious orders, the Knights of St John of Jerusalem, and the Knights Templar, who exercised probate jurisdiction. Although it passed into secular hands when the latter order was dissolved, the manorial lord retained probate jurisdiction.

Some peculiars were under secular jurisdiction. The Crown had a number of peculiars, for example St Buryan (Cornwall). So did a few manorial lords; the wills of Cockington (Devon) were proved in its manorial court. Some cities, for example London, Exeter, and Bristol, had orphans' courts which administered the goods of deceased citizens. The probate courts of the

Universities of Oxford and Cambridge had jurisdiction over university members wherever they were, without geographical restriction.

The probate records of peculiars are normally found with the archives of the dignitaries who had jurisdiction over them; for example, the Uffculme (Devon) records are amongst the archives of Salisbury Cathedral in Wiltshire and Swindon History Centre. That is fortunate; had they been held with other Exeter Diocesan probate records, they would have been destroyed by a German bomb in World War Two.

During the English Civil War and interregnum, the operation of ecclesiastical courts was first disrupted and then (temporarily) abolished. Between May 1643 and March 1646, the PCC sat in Oxford, where the Royalists held their court. In November 1644, Parliament established a rival court in London. The activities of the Oxford court were ruled invalid by Parliament; executors who had used it were required to prove their wills again in London. If this was not done, there will be no registered will, although the original may still survive amongst the archives (PROB10/639-42), as the records of the two courts were merged in 1646.

A court sitting at Doctors' Commons. Copied from Wikimedia)

Most local courts ceased to operate by around 1650. The PCC was replaced by the secular 'Court for the Probate of Wills and the Granting of Administrations' in 1653. The latter ceased to function in 1659, and the PCC was re-established in the following year. All the interregnum records are in English, and were merged with PCC records after 1660.

In the North, the expense of proving a will in London led some executors to avoid the interregnum court. A number of wills were executed without formal probate; others were proved in PCY after the Restoration, and are now held by the Borthwick Institute **www.york.ac.uk/library/borthwick** in York.

When Charles II was restored to the throne in 1660, the old system of church government was restored with him, together with its numerous ecclesiastical probate courts. The proliferation of courts means that probate records for particular individuals and places must be sought in a variety of places. County record offices do not necessarily hold all the wills relating to their counties. Many Shropshire wills, for example, must be sought in Lichfield (Staffordshire). A full list of probate courts, and of the record offices which hold their archives, is given in Appendix 1.

Executors and Administrators

The process of probate was begun by the executor as soon as the testator had died. It was his or her duty to carry out the wishes of the testator, and to distribute the estate in accordance with the will. He (or sometimes she), with witnesses, took the will to a probate court, and swore to its genuineness. Sometimes, in order to avoid long journeys, executors were sworn before local clergymen commissioned by the court. If the executor satisfied the court, he was granted probate: that is, permission to administer the estate. That permission would be recorded in the court's act book, where one was kept. In most courts, the will itself was annotated (in Latin before 1733) with a note of the grant of probate (which included certification of the executor's oath – the jurat), and filed amongst the court's records. A copy was given to the executor. This procedure was not invariable. In Lichfield Diocese, act books ceased to record grants of probate after 1638; instead, a slip of paper noting the names of the executors was filed with the original wills. Elsewhere, the will was copied into a register, and the original was handed back to the executor. In the PCC, the original will was retained by the court, but the executor could pay for it to be copied into the court's register of wills, as well as for a transcript for his or her own use. Original wills were loose documents; consequently, their survival rate is not as high as that of will registers.

Ideally, the original will is to be preferred to the registered copy. Registered wills are copies. They are therefore liable to errors made by the copyist. For

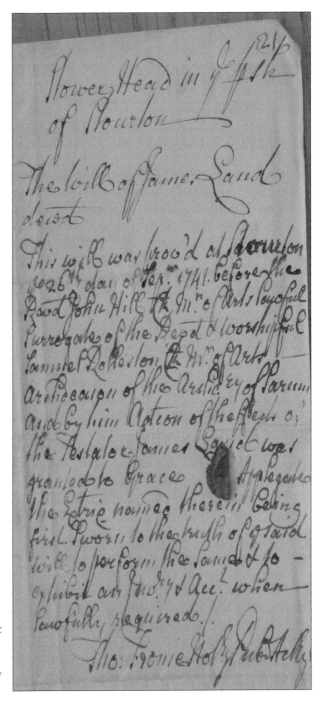

Note of probate on the back of James Land of Stourton's will, 1741.
(Wiltshire & Swindon History Centre P2/L/629)

example, when the will of Bartholomew Edwards of Stourton (Wiltshire) was registered in PCC in 1784, the scribe omitted an entire line, which appointed his brother, William Edwards of Clapham, as his executor. The line was subsequently written in on the side of the register. The handwriting of original wills may be worth study. Testators' and witnesses' signatures are likely to be genuine, and, as has been seen, are therefore of value to the student of literacy.

An act of 1529, which will be considered further below, required the court to act with 'convenient speed without any frustratory delay'. Probate was frequently granted within a few weeks of death. PCC took longer, as it could take time to organize a trip to London. Nevertheless, probate was usually granted within three months, and the administration of most estates (except, sometimes, those which were left to minors) was usually completed within a year.

It was not always possible for the court to grant probate to an executor. Some executors died before testators. Others did not feel equal to the task, or were not prepared to undertake it. Renunciations by executors can occasionally be found amongst probate records. Another problem for the probate court was posed by the testator who failed to name an executor. In all these cases, the court had to appoint an administrator, who was expected to carry out the provisions of the will.

If there was no will, it was up to the probate court to appoint an administrator. Normally, it only did so if administration was applied for. In many cases, no such application was made, and consequently no probate records were created. In some cases, estates were distributed before death, rendering letters of administration redundant. It was not, however, unknown for apparitors to cite executors who had failed to apply for probate, or for churchwardens to present them. Occasionally, courts granted administration for a limited portion of the estate, or a limited period of time. Such grants were sometimes recorded separately.

The act of 1529 required the court to grant letters of administration to the widow/widower, children, parents, siblings, next of kin, creditors or others, in that order, 'as by the discretion of the ordinary shall be thought good'. If no such person could be found, and if no heir could be identified, the estate was *bona vacantia* (see below), and reverted to the Crown.

Letters of administration do not normally survive, as they were granted to administrators rather than being kept in the probate court's archive. Grants of administration were, however, recorded in act books. An alternative record is provided by the bonds which administrators were usually required to sign (and which can frequently be found attached to inventories or wills). These imposed a financial penalty on administrators who failed in their duty to 'well and truely administer the estate'. Such bonds required two sureties. The first of these was usually a relative or close associate.

28

By the eighteenth century, the second was frequently a court official, or even the fictitious 'John Doe'. For a typical bond, see p. 64 below. The duties of administrators were identical to the duties of executors. They had to begin by swearing an oath to 'well and truly' administer the estate. Sometimes they were sworn by local clergymen commissioned by the court for the purpose. Administrators were expected to arrange for an inventory of the deceased's chattels to be compiled, to pay debts and legacies, to wind up the estate, and to submit to the court an account of their administration. The Lambeth Council of 1261 established the requirement for executors to prepare inventories, although this may have regularized an earlier practice. It was not until the statute of 1529, however, that inventories became common.

Inventories served as a check on executors and administrators, and facilitated payment of the deceased's debts. Most were compiled by neighbours and/or kin, although experts might be called on if there were specialized goods to value. In the Telford (Shropshire) area, for example, Alan Pickering was frequently called on for advice on the value of horses between 1680 and 1742. Mercers were likely to be called upon to value the stock of mercers; booksellers to value books. Occasionally, creditors carried out the valuation. Parish officers could also be involved. After 1670, the date for submission of the inventory was set in the administration bond. Usually, but not invariably, three months were allowed for the inventory. Frequently, however, the inventory was compiled within a few days of the deceased's death, and submitted to the court when probate was applied for.

Once the grant of probate had been made, estates were frequently wound up very quickly. However, there could be complications. Legal challenges might lead to considerable delay, especially if both ecclesiastical and secular courts were involved. The collection of debts might be problematic. So might the payment of creditors if there was not enough money available from the estate. The need to provide for orphans could entangle executors for years.

Probate accounts provide valuable evidence for the process of winding up estates. They were legally required from both executors and administrators, although in practice relatively few were actually exhibited. Under the act of 1670, the date for submission was set in the administration bond. They were required in order to make the affairs of the decedent public, to demonstrate that all debts had been paid, and to define the amount of the estate that was available for distribution amongst legatees. Accounts record payments made out of the estate for legal and funeral expenses, for the debts of the deceased, for the running of his estate, and for legacies paid. They represent the final stage in the process of probate. Once the evidence they provided had satisfied the court, the estate could be formally wound up.

Probate inventories survive in large numbers, especially between *c.*1550 and *c.*1750. There are far fewer probate accounts, and very few indeed after 1685. It has been estimated that only 30,000 are extant, compared to the millions of wills available. In Lichfield Diocese between 1679 and 1684, there were 581 grants of probate, and 420 letters of administration, but only 127 accounts were exhibited. This seems to have been fairly typical, although no accounts survive for Westmorland, and many thousand are available for Kent. This is unfortunate; where they survive they can provide valuable information to the inquirer.

Not everyone made a will. And not everyone had relatives to inherit their estate. If there was no lawful heir, and no one who could be appointed as administrator, the administration of the estate would be undertaken by the Treasury Solicitor, and it would revert to the Crown. For details of current arrangements, visit:

- **www.bonavacantia.gov.uk**.

Most records relating to *bona vacantia* are from the twentieth century; however, there are some records dating back to the seventeenth century in TNA, and especially in TS17. The pedigrees of some claimants to estates thought to be *bona vacantia* can be found in TS33; there are some letter books and other papers for the early nineteenth century in TS8 and TS9, and royal warrants and Treasury authorities to release estates to claimants can be found in TS30.

Chapter 3

WHAT CAN I FIND IN A WILL?

Michael Henchard's Will
That Elizabeth-Jane Farfrae be not told of my death, or made to grieve on
    account of me
& that I be not bury'd in consecrated ground
& that no sexton be asked to toll the bell
& that nobody is wished to see my dead body,
& that no murners walk behind me at my funeral,
& that no flours be planted on my grave
& that no man remember me
To this I put my name.

Thomas Hardy *The Mayor of Casterbridge*, Chapter 45

Personal Documents

Wills allow us to look into the minds of our predecessors, and observe
their thoughts, attitudes, and beliefs, in a way that no other source permits.
They are perhaps the most personal documents available for most of our
ancestors, and record the names of many of their contemporaries – not
just relatives, but also friends, neighbours, creditors, and others. They
also sometimes provide vivid descriptions of their possessions. Testators
knew their own possessions better than the appraisers of their inventories,
and sometimes provided more detailed descriptions. Consequently, wills
can sometimes be more useful than inventories; as we shall see, they
frequently provide much more information about clothing and costume
than is given in inventories.

The amount of information provided does, however, vary considerably.
The words 'All to wife' would be a perfectly valid will, provided that an
executor was named, and the document the words were written on was
properly signed and witnessed. Wills can sometimes be very brief. On the
other hand, they can also run to many pages, make many bequests, name
numerous people, and provide much information about the personality, the
family, and the goods, of the testator.

31

Testators

The name, parish, and perhaps the occupation or status of the testator is usually given close to the beginning of wills. Students should not assume that the spelling of the name is necessarily the spelling that is used in other sources, and it is worth comparing it with the testator's signature (which may have a quite different spelling). Uniformity of spelling was not a characteristic of any period before Dr Johnson wrote his dictionary, or, indeed, until the mid-nineteenth century.

The place of residence is likely to be useful information for the family historian. Frequently, just the parish is given, although this is not invariable. The names of farms and cottages do sometimes appear.

Wills frequently state the occupation of the testator. In Northampton between 1462 and 1509, this information is available in 120 out of 145 wills. A wide variety of status and occupational terms are used in wills. A study of status terms, such as 'husbandman' or 'yeoman', is likely to show how their meaning changed over the years. A man identified as a husbandman in the sixteenth century may have been equivalent in status to a yeoman in the eighteenth century, or even a gentleman. Students should compare the status or occupation of a testator as given in his will with the status or occupation as given in his inventory. They are not necessarily identical. In early eighteenth-century Worcestershire, six men who described themselves as gentlemen in their wills were described as husbandmen by their appraisers. On the other hand, ten who described themselves as husbandmen were identified as yeomen in their inventories. A will shows what a testator thought of himself; the inventory shows what his neighbours thought of him.

Occupational and status terms are not necessarily given in both will and inventory, a fact which demonstrates the importance of using them together. The probate records for Thomas Rastell of Birmingham, who died in 1591, again demonstrate the importance of using both will and inventory together. Rastell's inventory mentions quantities of cloth in the 'chamber over the hall', revealing that he was probably involved in some way in the cloth industry. But it states no occupation. His will states that he was a draper. Similarly, the inventory of Richard Chestlen of Foleshill (Warwickshire) lists his hammers, bellows, tongs, vices, and other tools, without stating his occupation explicitly. His will states what could only otherwise be inferred: he was a blacksmith.

Dates

Wills could be written at any time. The date is usually given in either the first or the last paragraph. It should be noted and compared with the date of burial in the parish register. Wills were usually written no longer than a week or so before the testator's death. Where that was not the case, the will may not reflect family births, marriages and deaths that occurred in the intervening period. The date of the will should also be compared with the date of probate, and the dates of inventories or accounts. This will help to reveal the process of probate at work. Bear in mind that before 1752 the year commenced on 25 March, not on 1 January.

In some cases, wills were written after death. Some testators did not have time to summon a scribe in order to write their will before they died. Instead, they spoke it in the presence of witnesses, who were prepared to testify to its content, and who caused a scribe to write it down after death. These are termed nuncupative wills.

If there is a gap between the date of the will and the date of death, it is likely that the testator had a specific reason. Sometimes, that reason is expressed in the will. Testators like Deryk Leke (see above, p. 18) who were going on a long journey, or attempting some other hazardous enterprise, might make a will first. Most, however, left the task of will-making until they knew that death was fast approaching.

There is another reason why the date of a will may be important. If the testator actually wrote several wills, the earlier documents would have been void as soon as the later ones were written. Testators did have an alternative to voiding a will. It could easily be amended by adding a codicil, or even two or three. If properly witnessed, such codicils were treated by probate courts as if they were part of the original will. Such codicils may record a wide variety of changes in circumstances. In 1630, for example, Dame Elizabeth Freville of Walworth (Co. Durham) added a codicil to her will ordering 10s to be distributed to the poor of Heighington every fortnight for up to twelve months 'in consideracion of the dearth & scarcity that is like to ensue this present yeare'.

The will is likely to describe the testator as 'weak in body'. If he were not, the will probably would not have been written. The words 'but perfect in memory', which may continue the sentence, affirm that the testator is legally competent to make the will.

Religious Clauses

Prior to the nineteenth century, many wills commenced with the words 'In the name of God', and proceeded directly to a bequest of the soul and an expression of religious faith. These words purport to represent the beliefs of the testator, but are quite likely to be formulaic. If so, they merely tell us that the scribe knew how to write a conventional will. The testator, unless he had particularly strong religious convictions, would be likely to leave these clauses to the scribe. If that was the case, they reflect the scribe's opinion (or merely the opinion of the formulary from which the scribe took his wording), not the testator's. Scribes who wrote several wills usually used the same wording. We should ascribe particular beliefs to testators, rather than scribes, only when there are unique expressions of faith, or the testator makes bequests for religious purposes.

The will of Thomas Belamy of London, written in 1518, is typical of pre-Reformation wills: he left his soul to 'Allmyghty God, to our Blissid Lady Sancte Mary, and to all the sainctes in hevyn'. The wording is merely formulaic, and inserted routinely by the scribe. John Kendalle, one of his fellow citizens, went further; he left 18s in 1516 'as alms to poor people to pray for the health of my soul'. He meant what he said. But both wills reflected popular belief of the times. Belief in purgatory was frequently evidenced by bequests of intercessory masses, donations to religious houses, and payments to chantry clergy. Their purpose was to reduce the period of time to be spent in purgatory. The onset of the Reformation, and especially official opposition to belief in purgatory, meant that such legacies rapidly ceased to be made. They could not be enforced in the face of official prohibition.

After the Reformation, scribes preferred formulae such as 'my sole to almighty God my maker and redeemer'. More fervent Protestants added more details of their faith, perhaps referring to the merits of Jesus Christ, assurance of salvation, and the doctrines of election and predestination. In 1665, George Roiston of Clayworth (Nottinghamshire) gave his soul

> into the hands of almighty God my creator my saviour and most mercifull father wholely reposing my soul upon his infinite mercies for the pardon of all my sinns and eternal salvation for the alone merits and mediation of my blessed lord saviour and redeemer Jesus Christ.

Such proclamatory bequests should be taken seriously. Someone – perhaps the testator, perhaps the scribe – genuinely held the beliefs proclaimed. They do reflect, at least to a degree, the strength of particular beliefs.

Religious preambles have proved to be of great interest to ecclesiastical historians, who have attempted to use them to trace the growth of Protestantism and the decline of Roman Catholicism. Wills which mention the Virgin Mary and the Saints are presumed to be Roman Catholic; those which mention the elect and predestination are considered to be Calvinistic. The use of these statements to determine belief is, however, problematic. They are likely to reflect scribes' opinions (or merely the wording of a formulary), rather than the opinions of testators. Nevertheless, that wording does illustrate common beliefs, as well as the (probable) beliefs of scribes. There is therefore some justification for analysing them to trace the spread of Protestant and Calvinistic ideas.

The changing religious wording used in wills also reflects to some indeterminate extent the reaction of individuals to government decrees. Testators (and their scribes) wanted their wills to be sound in law, and therefore used wording which would be acceptable to the authorities. After the Reformation, there was little point in making bequests that fell foul of the law against 'superstitious uses', It ceased to be sensible to request prayers for one's soul by will, since they were banned by law.

The penalties for failure to comply with religious requirements – Protestant or Papist – could be drastic. At least one testator who used the wrong wording in his will had his body exhumed and burnt at the stake! The unfortunate testator was a prominent Gloucestershire JP, William Tracy, who expressed his belief in justification by faith in 1530 – at a date when this was still a heretical belief. His refusal to make any bequests to the clergy may have exacerbated his heresy in the eyes of the probate court, and, eventually, of Convocation, with the consequence just mentioned. He was treated as a martyr by the Reformers, and his will was published. It is probable that it was used as a will formulary by the faithful. The same fate did not befall Peter Carter of Shincliffe (Co. Durham), who in 1588 bequeathed his 'sowle to almightie god and to all the holy company of Sainctes in heaven', over thirty years after the Protestant Elizabeth had come to the throne. By then, Tracy's phraseology had become the norm, and Carter's had become officially heretical. The end of the phrase was circled by a probably disapproving official of the court, but we know of no other action being taken.

These two wills evidently reflected the beliefs of the testators. That was not always the case. Willingham (Cambridgeshire) was a hotbed of Puritanism in the seventeenth century. It had a strong Congregationalist church during the interregnum, and there was also some Quaker influence. Its Puritanism could not, however, be deduced from the wills of parishioners. There are serious limits to what the religious clauses of wills can tell us.

The bequest of the soul is frequently accompanied by a request for burial in a particular place, or in a particular manner. John Long of Chesterfield (Derbyshire) requested that 'he die without anye manner of funerall pompe or other suche like unnecessarye charge whatsoever'. Others might request burial close to a relative. For example, in 1641, John Carter of Kings Langley asked 'to be buried in the Church of Kings Langly ... Neare unto the grave of John Carter my layt father'. A remarkable example of a request for burial is contained in the will of the Huguenot John Deschamp of Twickenham. He asked initially to be buried in the church of St Marylebone. However, his body was to be moved subsequently so that he could lie with his widow when she died, wherever she might be buried. Not only that, but he then named no fewer than twelve other relatives, ranging from his grandparents to his daughter, whose bodies were to be moved with his!

Bequests of the body may tell you where to look for burial records, monumental inscriptions, and other records, and may also (as in the case of John Deschamp) provide direct linkage to other family members. The place mentioned may be where the testator was born, or where he had family connections. For the local historian, such clauses help to provide the evidence needed to study the mobility of the local population. If the testator asks to be buried inside a church, that is a clear indicator of wealth or status.

The main body of a will consists of bequests. These frequently commence with religious donations, reflecting the ecclesiastical origins of will-making. The fabric of local churches benefited from the wills of local people, especially before the Reformation. Many such gifts were lost at the hands of the reformers, and such bequests almost ceased after the mid-sixteenth century. Fervent Protestants were more likely to leave bequests for 'lecturers' – preachers – who would proclaim the Gospel in regular sermons, supplementing the work of the local clergy. After the Restoration in 1660, religious bequests were sometimes redirected to Nonconformist causes. For example, in 1701, John Moores left £5 to 'the poore Friends belonging to Hertford Meeting', and a further £5 to be distributed amongst 'any poore Ministry Friends that travells this way for the service of Truth'.

Bunhill Fields: a Nonconformist burial ground. (Courtesy of Dr Neil Clifton)

Wills are a prime source for the history of charities, and have been extensively used for this purpose by W.K. Jordan. See, for example, his *Philanthropy in England 1480–1640: a study of the changing pattern of social aspirations* (G. Allen & Unwin, 1959). Bequests to the poor were encouraged by churchmen on both sides of the Reformation divide – although in Week St Mary (Cornwall) they went into steep decline during the seventeenth century. In 1681, Thomas Boothby left his house 'to the use of the poore of Winteringham [Lincolnshire] being of what religion or persuasion whatsoever'; his trustees were to let it and distribute the rent to the poor as they thought fit. The trustees, like the testator, were Quakers, as were their successors.

Charitable bequests frequently went beyond a simple bequest to the poor. Many wills established almshouses, hospitals, and schools, or made other provision. In Exeter, for example, bequests established several charities to apprentice poor children.

Most bequests were made to kin, usually to wives and children. The range of kin mentioned did not usually go much beyond the nuclear family. Nieces and nephews were sometimes mentioned: James Pendred of Hertford left £25 each to the four children of his brother John in 1701 – but he could not remember their names! More distant kin rarely received legacies. Nor did neighbours and friends, although occasionally servants were remembered.

The Process of Inheritance

Testators were likely to mention all surviving children. Bequests to them were not necessarily all that they might seem. They must be placed in their wider context if we are to understand their meaning. Wills illuminate a particular moment in time, when testators were preparing to leave this world. They do not necessarily record all the arrangements which had been made to provide for testators' heirs. Inheritance was a process, not a single event. It did not depend solely upon wills. A will was merely one step in the process, which was likely to begin with the marriage of the eldest son, and to end with the death of the widow, or the coming of age of the youngest child.

Fathers did not wait until their deathbeds to ensure the livelihoods of their children. They would pay out good money to apprentice their sons to a trade, or to marry off their daughters. Sons might be given their own holdings long before their father died. Thomas Appleby of Thornton Curtis (Lincolnshire) established four of his sons and a daughter with cash gifts of £150 each before he died, leaving his fifth son to be paid his promised portion by his widow. Almost half of the resources bestowed by Ralph Josselin, the vicar of Earls Colne (Essex), on his children were given well before his death. It cost him £100 to apprentice his son Thomas; eight years later, he gave him another £50 to stock his shop. He gave his daughters, between them, £800 in cash, and another £400 in lands, for their marriage portions, but only £500 of this was given by will. Josselin's diary shows the process of inheritance as it actually happened.

The eldest son would normally inherit his father's landed property under the rules of primogeniture. In some places, local custom dictated otherwise. The custom of gavelkind (equal division amongst sons) was common in Kent. Borough English (descent to the youngest son) was frequently found in the south-east and other areas. As realty was outside of the jurisdiction of the ecclesiastical courts, it might not be mentioned in the will. Many testators were content to allow the law of inheritance to take its course.

Some, however, were not. Testators sometimes spelt out in detail how their property was to descend. In 1670, Michael Hartshorne of Clayworth (Nottinghamshire) left his farm to his son Anthony and to his heirs. If there were no such heirs, the property was to descend 'to my sonne John Hartshorne and the heires of his body begotton or to be begotton. And for want of such heires then to Mary Barker my daughter'.

The purpose of wills was frequently to provide for younger children who had not already been provided for, and to ensure that widows were looked after in their old age. A son who received a shilling in his father's will was not usually being cut out of his inheritance; rather, he had already been established in his livelihood, and the shilling was a mere token of recognition. Nicholas King of Kings Langley, when he made his will in 1599, was primarily concerned to make substantial bequests to his wife and four younger sons. His eldest son was named executor and residuary legatee, but is not otherwise mentioned. We know from other sources that he inherited the bulk of his father's property, and that two other sons, unusually not mentioned in the will at all, had probably received considerable help from their father to establish themselves as farmers of substantial demesne lands.

Testators took particular care in making provision for minors, who were frequently apprenticed if they became orphans. Elizabeth Wawen of Clayworth (Nottinghamshire) left her son Robert £40. Some £30 of this was to be spent on paying his apprenticeship premium, and the remainder on clothes for his apprenticeship. His master was also expected to provide clothing; he was to be paid 20s per annum for this purpose. Robert was also to be given a bed and bedding when he had completed his term.

Testamentary provision for married daughters was frequently minimal – they had already received their portions. Unmarried daughters, however, had to be married off. Legacies focused on their marriage. Conditions were frequently imposed. John Leigh of Week St Mary (Cornwall) warned his daughters that 'if they be not ruled' by his trustees, 'in marining (sic) into an honest family and deserving of there portion', they would have 'no benefit of ye said portion except they stand in want for food or reiment'. Elizabeth Neale of Banbury (Oxfordshire) left her daughter £10, on condition that she married Christopher Ingraham. Her refusal to do so reduced her legacy by half.

Perhaps the over-riding consideration for married will-makers was the need to provide for their widows. Widows frequently came last in the poverty stakes, and men felt under a strong sense of obligation to make adequate provision for them. In doing so, they frequently expressed their regard for their wives, and gave the lie to the idea that affection in marriage was rare in early modern England. For example, in 1621 James West of Banbury, yeoman, said of his wife that she had

> alwaies carried here self as a very loving and dutifull wife to me, being a speciall meanes by her good huswyfrie, painfulnes and diligent walkinge in her calling to raise that estate the Lord hath blessed us withall.

Robert Beilby of Selby, whose will was proved in 1704, devised the messuage where he lived, which he had purchased from his brother Thomas Hodgson, jointly to Alice 'my beloved wife' and to Rebeckah, 'my youngest daughter'. He also made them joint executors and residuary legatees, 'it being my desire that they live together in Love & Charity & be assistant one to the other in managing the trade of Pipe-making for an honest livelihood'.

If there was limited provision for a widow in a will, this may have been due to the fact that she was entitled to a proportion – frequently a third – of her husband's real estate, settled on her when she married. Otherwise, bequests to widows could be quite elaborate. George Leigh of Week St Mary (Cornwall) gave his wife a part of his house at Groves End, together with rights of way, 'commons' in the town place, liberty to bake, brew, and make malt, and to take fuel. She was also given corn, beasts, beds, and household equipment. William Blake, another Week St Mary testator, made provision in case his wife and his son did 'not agree to lyve and keepe howse together'.

Testators were alive to the problems that their widows might encounter. In 1668, Richard Goulden of Bowden (Cheshire) left £5 to his brother Thomas, but ordered 'that if my brother . . . bee not peaceable and quiat with Jane my wife that then [he] shall loose his above said five pounds and bee cut off with twelve pence'.

Many bequests to widows were for life only, and were to revert to children on her death. Very occasionally, testators stipulated that legacies would be forfeit if their widows remarried. John Saunders of Week St Mary gave his widow 'the use . . . of all my said goods . . . with my house ground and garden as longe as shee remaineth a widdow . . . and noe longer'. If she remarried, she was to have only her clothing (which were *bona paraphernalia*, and therefore hers anyway).

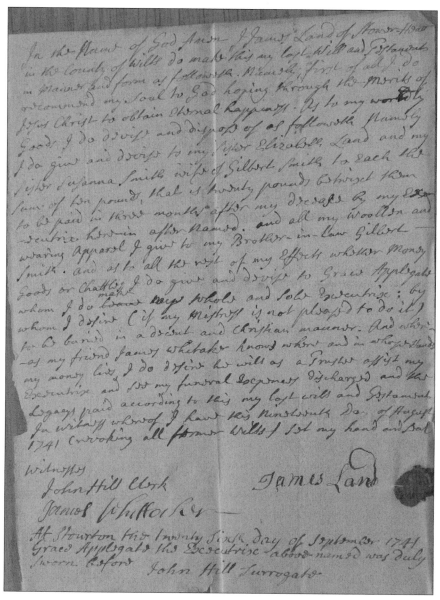

The Will of James Land of Stourhead, Wiltshire, 1741. (Wiltshire & Swindon Archives P2/L/629)

Transcript:

In the Name of God Amen I James Land of Stower Head in the county of Wilts do make this my last Will and Testament in manner and form as followeth. Namely first of all I do recommend my soul to God hoping through the merits of Jesus Christ to obtain eternal happiness. As to my worldly Goods I do devise and dispose of as followeth Namely I do give and devise to my sister Elizabeth Land and my sister Susanna Smith wife of Gilbert Smith to each the sum of ten pounds, that is twenty pounds betwixt them to be paid in three months after my decease by my executrix hereinafter named. and all my wollen and wearing apparel I give to my Brother-in-law Gilbert Smith. and as to all the rest of my effects whether Money Goods or Chattels I do give and devise to Grace Applegate whom I do ~~leave~~ make[1] my whole and sole executrix: by whom I desire (if my Mistress is not pleased to do it) to be buried in a decent and Christian manner. And whereas my friend James Whitaker knows where and in whose Hands my money lies I do desire that he will as a Trustee assist my Executrix and see my funeral expenses discharged and the legacys paid according to this my last will and Testament In witness whereof I have this nineteenth day of August 1741 (revoking all former wills) set my hand and seal

James Land

Witnesses
　　　John Hill Clerk
　　　James Whittaker

At Stourton the twenty sixth day of September 1741 Grace Applegate the Executrix above named was duly sworn before

John Hill Surrogate

---

1. Interlined.

There was a good reason why a testator might limit his widow's rights in this way. On remarriage, a widow's property (including anything she had brought from her previous marriage) became her new husband's. He might be unwilling to comply with the terms of the testator's will, and could pose a serious threat to legacies intended for minors.

Widows had rather different considerations in mind when they wrote their wills. They seldom had to worry about securing their children's future, although their wills can be seen as another stage in the process of inheritance. Their deaths meant that children would inherit the lands bequeathed to them by their husbands for life. There may be a tendency for widows to favour their daughters in their bequests, and for a wider range of people to receive bequests – especially if there were no children to inherit. For Frances Saxton of Coulton (Yorkshire), the purpose of making a will was to

avoyd all sutes and Contencyons that in any mannor way may aryse or grow therupon for and aboute the same Betwixt my two Daughters after my decease.

After the bequests, testators normally name their executors, who are also usually their residuary legatees. A study of the names of executors, and of

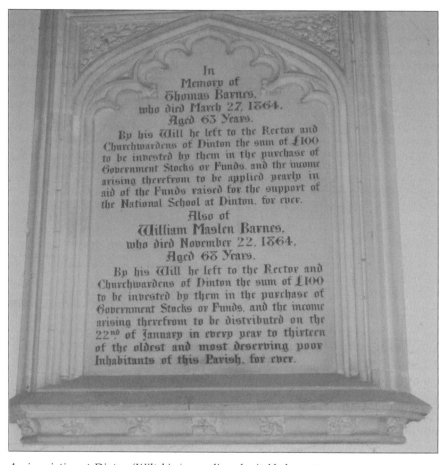

An inscription at Dinton (Wiltshire) recording charitable bequests.

their relationship to testators, reinforces the conclusion that has already been reached. Wills were primarily intended to provide for younger children, and for widows. Therefore, widows were frequently named as executrices. As Sir Thomas Smith observed, there were few widows

> that be not made at the death of their husbandes either sole or chiefe executrixes of his last wil and testament, and have for the most part the government of the children and their portions.

In late fifteenth-century Northampton, widows were named as executrices in all but two wills of married men. In Week St Mary (Cornwall), eldest sons who had younger siblings or surviving mothers were not named as executors in the seventeenth century. This rule was not, however, universal;

in sixteenth- and early seventeenth-century Kings Langley (Hertfordshire), executors were frequently eldest sons.

Sometimes, testators also named overseers. Their task was to ensure that executors fulfilled their obligations. They were commoner in some regions of the country than in others, and may have been used to thwart any attempt by executors to favour particular beneficiaries of the will over other beneficiaries. Step-mothers, for example, were likely to be suspected of favouring their own children over their step-children. It is likely that some step-mothers were deliberately excluded as executrices for this reason. Do not, incidentally, automatically assume that a widow was the mother of all the children named by a testator. Remarriage following the death of a spouse was common.

Signatures, Witnesses and Probate

Wills generally end with the signature of the testator, and of two or more witnesses. The role of the witnesses was to authenticate the will, and to guard against fraud. They could not be children, criminals, lunatics, or legatees. Again, the relationship of the witnesses to the testator could be important, and worth investigating. The signatures themselves provide useful evidence for the history of literacy.

Once a will had been proved, a note of the grant of probate (sometimes referred to as the 'probate clause') was written on it, sometimes at the foot, sometimes on its verso. These notes are formulaic, and merely note the date (and perhaps the place) of the grant, the name of the judge, and the name of the sworn executor. Until 1733 (except during the interregnum) these notes are in Latin.

Goods in Wills

Wills were statements of intent. It should not be assumed that executors received sufficient funds from estates to pay all legacies. A better indication of the wealth of a decedent can be found by consulting probate inventories and accounts. These documents should always be compared with each other. Whilst inventories should provide comprehensive lists of possessions, wills frequently add much detail. For example, where inventories simply refer to 'wearing apparel', wills may provide greatly expanded descriptions. 'Wearinge apparell' valued at 40s is listed in the Kings Langley inventory of William Rogers in 1540. His will, however, shows that he left his 'best suite of weareing apparell & one white hat' to his brother Richard, 'my second suite of apparell & my best blacke hat, and a paire of green silk garters' to his brother John, and 'all the rest of my wearinge apparell un-bequethed' to his father Richard. We have no inventory for Robert Yedaille of Gray's Inn, but we do know that in 1543 he left his brother 'my best gowne, my best capp, and my fyne woorsted dowblett', and his grandson 'my study gowne furred wythe black lam, my chamlett jakett, a kapp and a pare of hoose'. His sister-in-law received 'a gowne [and] clothe of puk'. Others were given 'myn old gowne furred wythe cony', 'myn old blak worsted coot and an old woorsted dowblett, myn old study gowne and my fustyan dowblett'. It is doubtful if this amount of detail would have been included by an appraiser.

Another reason to examine the goods bequeathed in wills is the fact that they are frequently not mentioned in inventories. It is probable that many were removed by legatees before the appraisers started work. There could be other reasons for these omissions from inventories. Henry Wright of Banbury left his son Martin 'my lycence for sellinge of wine' in 1617. It evidently did not occur to his appraisers to value this licence. Differences such as this may be informative. Wills and inventories, if used together, may be much more useful than if they are read separately.

Chapter 4

WHAT CAN I FIND IN A PROBATE INVENTORY?

It shall be inventoried,
And every particle and utensil labelled to my will,
As, item, two lips indifferent red,
Item, two grey eyes, with lids to them,
Item, one neck, one chin, and so forth

William Shakespeare, *Twelfth Night*

The History of Inventories

Probate inventories are lists of the goods and chattels in the possession of deceased persons at the time of their death, with valuations. The 20th canon of the 1261 Council of Lambeth required the production of *'de bonis defuncti fidele inventarium'* – a faithful inventory of the goods of the deceased. Despite this and other ecclesiastical attempts to enforce the requirement, only a modest number of medieval inventories survive. It was not until 1529, when they were required by statute, that they began to survive in substantial numbers. They continued to be made throughout the seventeenth century, but gradually ceased to be retained in court archives in the eighteenth century. In the PCC, they were not required after 1710, except when litigation took place. By contrast, in the peculiar of Ellesmere (Shropshire), they are found in the 1790s. The compilation of inventories in the Madeley (Shropshire) area suddenly ceased in 1762, suggesting that the Hereford Diocesan authorities had taken a definite decision to end the practice.

The fact that inventories were not retained does not necessarily mean that they were not made. Many probate act books and administration registers note the value of estates. So do the death duty registers (see below, Chapter 10). That valuation must have come from inventories. Executors and administrators needed to have them made to protect themselves, but preferred to avoid court fees if they could; they may not have bothered to

A box of inventories. (Courtesy of Dr Todd Gray)

register them. The courts may have felt that inventories were becoming more trouble than they were worth. Increasing wealth, and a rapidly increasing number of items to record in inventories, meant that their numbers were increasing and becoming bulkier. Probate clerks may have simply decided that they did not have the space to store them, other than in exceptional circumstances.

Appraisers and their Work

Inventories were usually compiled within a few days of death. The appraisers were appointed by executors or administrators. The act required that they be 'honest and skilful', and that they should be chosen from creditors, legatees or next of kin. If none of these was available, choice was to be made of 'two honest men'. In practice, appraisers were usually neighbours, although in the Southwell (Nottinghamshire) peculiar, one appraiser was frequently a member of the family. Southwell inventories frequently had three or four appraisers, more than is usually found. In some places, there were men who were regularly called on to appraise inventories, and who may have done so as professionals. John Hartshorne appraised at least sixty-three inventories in the Madeley (Shropshire) area in the early eighteenth century.

Occasionally, churchwardens and overseers sought to intervene in the process. When Michael Dix died in 1613, Banbury's parish officers went to his house in order to take an inventory, but were repulsed by his son-in-law. He 'withestonde us and denyed us the takinge and sayd that he woulld not tell us of Anye thinge that was Micahell Dyxe his good but that he will dow hit himsellfe'. The dead man had been responsible for a parish apprentice; the overseers were concerned that his son-in-law had 'cast her uppon us Agayne'.

The task of the appraisers was to list and value the goods of the deceased. Most people would not have found this a difficult task, since their own goods would have been fairly similar. The goods recorded in most inventories were not greatly differentiated from each other in terms of quality. Men knew what they would be willing to pay for tables and chairs, or fireside equipment. Most people kept their own livestock, and knew the value of a sheep or a pig. Nevertheless, Richard Burn, in his famous work *The ecclesiastical law* (4th ed., 1842, p. 418) emphasized the necessity for appraisers 'to competently understand the value of the deceased's goods'. If they did not, then they could call in experts who did. Trade goods, for example, might not be familiar to the average appraiser. The vats used by a dyer, or the stock of a bookseller, needed expert appraisal. Accounts (see Chapter 6) may reveal payments made to specialists brought in to value them.

Appraisers were supposed to make two copies of inventories, one for the court and one for the executor or administrator. The copies should have been written on the same sheet, and separated by cutting along an indented line. If any dispute arose, their authenticity could be proved by joining the two together again. However, it seems that this requirement was frequently ignored.

Accounts may also reveal payments made to scribes. Appraisers did not have to be literate; the inability to write did not affect their ability to value goods. Illiterate appraisers had to employ scribes. Sometimes scribes signed their names. If not, and they are not mentioned in accounts, it may be possible to identify them by comparing the handwriting with other probate documents from the same place and period.

Inventories begin by recording details of the deceased, including his occupation and/or status. The names of the appraisers, and possibly their parishes and occupations, follow. They usually sign at the foot of the inventory, so a study of their literacy is possible.

Probate inventory of James Lange of Week St Mary. (Cornwall Record Office AP/L/325)

Transcript:

The Inventorie of all the goods & chattells of James Lange late of weeke s[nt] marie[1] in the Countie of Cornwalle husbandman decesed & mary Lange wid decessed valued & praysed by Thomas Prust & Thomas Trewyne the xxiiiith day of Jully 1629 in maner & forme followinge

Impmis[2] theyre wearinge apparrell	xxs
It one chattell lease of one Burgage tenemt wth appurtencs[3] in weeke s[nt] mary aforesd	iiil vis
It one cowe & one yarlinge	xlvis viiid
It one old duste bedd & furniture[4]	vs
It one tabellborde	iiis iiiid
It one cubbord	vs
It one brassen pott & one littell panne	vs
It in pewter	iis
Item one old coffer	viiid

Thomas Prust
Thomas Trewine

1. Note the indiscriminate use of upper and lower case
2. Imprimis: note the abbreviation mark for 'ri'.
3. Appurtenances – abbreviated, but there is no abbreviation mark.
4. The 'furniture' was bed furniture, i.e. mattress, sheets, blankets etc.

Contents of Inventories

The main body of a probate inventory is a detailed description of such material goods as our ancestors possessed – table boards and stools, andirons and pot hangings, bedsteads and linen, with valuations. The inventory of James Lange (p. 48) shows how sparse possessions could sometimes be. Apart from his lease, the decedent had only a few scraps of furniture, a couple of pots and pans, and two animals. Yet many inventories were valued at less than this. In 1567, William Patteson, a labourer of Bedale (Yorkshire) had goods worth a mere £1 10s 7d. These inventories provide a great contrast to the inventory of John Hill of Stourton (Wiltshire), which can only be illustrated here in part (see p. 50–1). He had a great variety of beds and bedding; his kitchen was well equipped, and he had £20 10s in cash – more than the total of Lange's inventory. Hill described himself as a yeoman in his will, but in fact he was a mercer. The second page of his inventory (not illustrated here) shows that amongst his stock he had four quires of paper worth 7s 6d, sugar valued at £4, and six shillings worth of soap, together with cloth, buttons, salt, and a wide variety of other goods. He was worth altogether £308 10s 11d.

Appraisers' descriptions enable us to picture the environment in which our ancestors lived. The amount of detail given depended on the caprice of the appraiser. The inventory of Joyce Bradshaw of Sellington (Shropshire), compiled in 1687, shows that in her 'parlour chamber' she had 'a halfe headed bedstead', two blankets, one coverlet, one feather bed, one feather bolster, and one feather pillow. Other appraisers might have simply recorded 'beds and bedding'.

Some goods are much scarcer. In view of the fact that there was a Civil War in the mid-seventeenth century, it might have been expected that guns and armour would appear more frequently than they do. Only five of the 190 Lichfield inventories edited by Vaisey (covering the period 1568–1680) mention swords, with another three listing rapiers.

Musical instruments also appear infrequently: they were luxury items. Only two are mentioned in the inventories of Shakespeare's Stratford on Avon (Warwickshire).

Books mentioned in inventories were mostly relatively expensive items. The chapbooks which many would have been familiar with were usually considered too ephemeral to be worth valuing. Some of these may have been included amongst those listed in the inventory of Arthur Starkey of Wrenbury (Cheshire) in 1622; he had ten books 'whereof som be very ould and little worth' altogether valued at 10s. Many inventories simply give a round value for books, without mentioning titles. Of those titles which are listed, the Bible is frequently named, even in poorer communities. Richard Harrison, cathedral chancellor at Lichfield (Staffordshire), had a bible on

A Portion of the Inventory of John Hill of Gasper, Stourton, Wiltshire, 1711. (Actually, this portion of Stourton was in Somerset.) (Wiltshire & Swindon Archives P2/H/1092)

Transcript:

1. A true and perfect Inventory of all and singular the goods and chattles of John Hill late of Gasper [interlined] within the parish of Stourton in the County of Somerset yeoman [interlined] deceased taken and apraised the ninteenth day of September in the yeare of our Lord One Thousand Seven Hundered and Eleven by us whose names are hereunto Subscribed

Imp his wearing apparell valued att	5-00-00
Item in mony in howse	20-10-00
Item in mortgages bonds bills and book debts	135-01-00
Item in one chattle lease at 5^{li} per annum at 14 yeares purchase	70-00-00
Item in one chattle lease at 2^{li} per annum at 12 yeares purchase	24-00-00

In the Chamber over the Kitchine

Two feather beds two bedsteeds five blanketts two coverleds two coffers one Chest two boxes two trunks three chares five paire of sheets seven paire of pillow tyes eight bolster tyes two dozen of napkins two table cloaths five bolsters seven pillows one looking glasse all valued at	14-07-00

In the Chamber over the Buttery

One feather bed one flock bed two bed steeds five blanketts two ruggs one coverlead two chests two boxes one trunk one little table one clock halfe one hundred of cheese [interlined] all valued att	08-19-00

In the Kittchine

One long table one little table one dressing table five cook potes five kittles one posnett one skillett two formes five chaires two spitts five pair of pott hooks one warming pan one still foure paire of hangings one fire pan & tongues one paire of andirons two skimmers two beef forkes one baking ladle two guns one rack with bacon theron one paire of billows two smoothing irons thirteen pewter dishes eleven plates seven poringers one flaggon one tankard two candlestickes foure salts all valued at	10-17-00

In the Buttery

Eight barrells one silt one poudering tub three tubbs one brewing fate five trendles one frying pan two ranges one sarch one lanthorne two dozen & halfe of trenchers five trendles one washing tub three partes all valued att	5-00-00

In the Stayre Head

Two small caskes of brandy valued at	1-00-00

a stand, and a copy of Foxe's *Book of martyrs*, together worth 14s. It is surprising that a person in his position did not have more books (although these were the two most popular books of the day). The inventories of clergy record more titles than those of most decedents. In contrast to Harrison, the appraisers of Isaac Lowden, the vicar of Doncaster (Co. Durham), who died in 1612, effectively provided a catalogue of the books in his library. The detailed (and relatively rare) evidence of his inventory shows what puritanically-inclined seventeenth-century clergymen were reading, and how they were being influenced.

Lay people could also have many books. Dorothy Cotton of Combermere (Cheshire), had books valued at £3 6s 8d in her 1647 inventory. Her appraisers did not list them, but fortunately some can be identified in her will. They were mostly works of prominent Puritans, and show that she was a woman of considerable piety. She was also wealthy, with an inventory valued at £374 6s 8d.

Inventory listings of household goods show how empty our ancestors' houses were prior to the eighteenth century. They demonstrate that sixteenth- and seventeenth-century houses were for working in, sleeping in, and eating in. They were emphatically not for relaxing in. Inventories also reveal the changing contents of houses, and changing attitudes towards those contents. Household goods in many places (although not in all) are listed room by room, enabling us to reconstruct houses, and to see how rooms were used. For example, John Jones of Clifton (Gloucestershire) in 1636 had a shop, a west chamber, a middle chamber, a hall, and a kitchen. In 1668 Henry Brereton, the minister of Clifton, had an 'inward lower roome', a chamber over the kitchen, a chamber for the maid, a 'little chamber at the head of the stayres', a 'new chamber, a 'greate chamber', a room within the great chamber, and another above it, a kitchen, a buttery, an old kitchen, and a little buttery. He also had a study, with a desk and books worth £10.

In the eighteenth century, a much greater proportion of inventories identified separate rooms in houses than had been the case two centuries earlier. That in itself is probably a sign of increasing wealth. However, even if an inventory does give room names, it is not necessarily a straightforward task to reconstruct houses with their contents. Appraisers were not aiming to list every room in a house, but only those where the decedent had goods. Decedents may have only used one or two rooms in a much bigger house. And other people may have had goods in those same rooms. In Ipswich (Suffolk), it has been estimated that less than half of the published inventories record all the rooms in the houses where decedents lived. In some places, appraisers did not mention rooms at all: it has already been seen that they are totally absent from the seventeenth-century inventories of Week St Mary (Cornwall).

Very occasionally, it is possible to find two inventories, or even more, relating to the same house. These can be compared to show the changing pattern of room use, or perhaps alterations made to the house. If the decedents are related, as is likely to be the case, they may also throw light on each other's affairs. The Lichfield (Staffordshire) inventories of William Thorneworke and Richard Reade, for example, were made in 1673, but give a completely different impression of the same house. Both had been married to Anne, who chose to apply for administration for both her husbands on the same day. Their goods were quite distinct, but seem to have been in the same house at the same time. Consequently, neither gives a true impression of the contents of the house: they have to be read together.

It may also be possible to identify inventories for houses that are still standing. This is uncommon; out of 265 inventories for Banbury (Oxfordshire) between 1591 and 1659, only two could be matched with modern houses with a reasonable degree of confidence. However, very detailed estate records in Stoneleigh (Warwickshire) enabled Nick Alcock (*People at home: living in a Warwickshire parish*, Phillimore, 1993) to match inventories to many surviving houses. It may also be possible to compare the number of rooms listed in inventories with hearth tax assessments, which are based on the number of hearths.

Kine and sheep, pigs and horses, and all the other domesticated livestock owned by our ancestors, are also listed. So are the crops in both field and barn. Then there are the pack saddles, the dungcarts, the ploughs, and other agricultural equipment around the farmyard. Buildings in the yard, such as stables and barns, may also be mentioned. John Miller of Leigh (Dorset) in 1690 had five 'milch cowes', four heifers, three calves, a mare and a colt, ten hogs, and two swine. His agricultural equipment include a cart and wheels, a dung pot, and two eithes (light harrows), together with an iron bar, two shovels, and a spade. He also had wood 'in the barton', that is, in the farmyard. Bartholomew Royle of Foleshill (Warwickshire) in 1564 had corn and hay in the barn worth 40s.

The inventories of tradesmen and craftsmen are likely to list the goods they had for sale, and the tools they used in practising their trades. Sometimes appraisers were very terse. John Dombelton was Banbury's wheelwright when he died in 1604. 'Hys workyng tools' were valued at 7s, but no other information is given. Other inventories, however, provide much detail. Mercers' inventories, for example, are likely to be full of fabrics such as cambrics, hollands and fustians. They also stocked groceries, together with general ware such as the 'potts, glasses, bottelles, pitch and tarre and hoppes and soap' which the appraisers of Richard Showell's Banbury inventory valued at £10 in 1611. In 1635, another Banbury tradesman, Thomas Pedlie, a shoemaker, had twenty pairs of 'unsaleable shooes' worth £1. Why they were unsaleable we are left to guess. A blacksmith's inventory will usually list his anvil and other smithing tools: Henry Goff of Westerleigh (Gloucestershire) had two pairs of bellows, a pair of tongs, a shovel, a large anvil, a small anvil, and various other tools, altogether worth over £8. The appraisers of the fishermen of Clee (Lincolnshire) frequently listed their boats and nets. Henry Mason, for example, who died in 1540, owned a part of a boat worth 10s. Tradesmens' inventories may also reveal how much they charged their customers. The Earl of Arlington, for example, owed Thomas Shave, shoemaker of Newmarket (Suffolk) 32s for 'two payre of bootes'. Inventories offer much potential for research in the history of particular trades.

Inventory valuations are usually reasonably accurate in terms of sales potential. It is, however, a mistake to assume that average inventory valuations reflect market values. Goods and livestock sent to market would have been in marketable condition. Inventoried goods and livestock were not necessarily in that condition. The valuation of crops and livestock would also have depended on the season of the year. Crops already sent to market would not have been valued.

Care must be taken in accepting appraisers' arithmetic calculations. Their skills were not always equal to the task of addition. It has been calculated by Steer, in his *Farm and cottage inventories of mid-Essex, 1635–1749* (2nd ed., Phillimore, 1969) that a third of inventories in Writtle and Roxwell were given incorrect totals.

The language used in inventories also requires care in interpretation. It is not modern English, and not necessarily easy to penetrate. Many items that an appraiser would have assumed to be familiar are no longer household objects. We no longer use andirons to support logs in the fireplace, nor do we use leather bottles to carry cyder to the harvest-field. Some words are obsolete; others have completely different meanings today. A ladder, for example, could have been framework on the sides or back of a wain to hold in large loads of hay. Furniture did not have its present-day meaning; rather, a 'bed with all its furniture' was a bed that was fully set up, with pillows, mattresses, sheets, etc. Other words could have a variety of different meanings. A horse could be an animal for riding or pulling carts, but it could also be a stand for barrels, trestles, or a wooden framework for drying clothes. It is important to be aware of the context in which such words appear; otherwise they may be misinterpreted. The present author's *Words from wills and other probate records 1500–1800: a glossary* (FFHS, 2006) attempts to define words that are commonly found.

Inventories are invaluable sources for recreating the material culture of our ancestors. They can, however, be deceptive. Not everything was included. It should not be assumed that all inventories necessarily recorded complete estates. If creditors took on responsibility for administration, they might only value sufficient goods to pay the decedent's debts. Sometimes goods were removed before the inventory was compiled. Most of the clothes mentioned by Margaret Justice of Newport (Shropshire) in her 1687 will were not listed in her inventory, presumably because they had been removed by legatees before the appraisers started their work. Freehold and copyhold land, although it might be left by will, was not subject to the ecclesiastical courts, and was therefore not listed in inventories, despite the fact that it

54

was frequently the most valuable asset that testators had. Appraisers were not expected to concern themselves with goods that testators had given away in their own lifetimes, and which were actually in the possession of recipients.

Inventories which *only* include leases present a different problem. If a burial is not apparent from the parish register, it may well be that the inventory was exhibited by a descendant many years after the decedent's death. In such cases, that descendant's right to inherit the lease may have been challenged. Exhibiting the inventory may have been one way of proving that right. Such inventories should not be regarded as full inventories. The appraisers would not concern themselves with other goods which had been dispersed, except perhaps using the catch-all phrase, 'things forgot'.

One way of identifying omissions in an inventory is to examine its internal logic. If it does not mention beds, where did the testator sleep? If a yeoman had crops but no farming equipment, what did he use for plough-ing and reaping? Overton et al, in their *Production and consumption in English households, 1600–1750* (Routledge, 2004) have developed the use of regression analysis to predict the presence or absence of particular goods in inventories. Whilst this is only for the mathematically inclined, it is reasonable to argue that the absence of an item from an inventory is not, in itself, sufficient reason to assume that the decedent did not have that item.

It is important to appreciate that there were a wide range of legal exclusions. The law was complex, and sometimes open to different inter-pretations. Standards of living were rising, goods were becoming more diversified, agricultural practices were changing, and new goods such as tea and tobacco were challenging the interpretation of the law. The probate status of goods without resale value, debts, leases, and fixtures, were all fluid. It was not always easy to draw the line between what should be included, and what should be excluded. Even leading contemporary textbooks, such as the many editions of Burn's *Ecclesiastical law*, were not always certain.

Goods that had no resale value included, most prominently, food. Only stored food such as meat was listed. Food that was about to be consumed was perishable, and had very limited monetary value. It was rarely mentioned. The only food in the 1567 inventory of John Thornhill of Flixby (Yorkshire) was 'one galon of hony', worth 2s 4d, found in his buttery. A victualler might be expected to have some food in his house, but Thomas Pearce, victualler, of Kings Langley (Hertfordshire), had only apples worth 2s when he died in 1626. Goods such as tea, tobacco, and sugar are usually only found in the inventories of merchants and traders who had them for sale.

Clothes were worth a little more, but are generally poorly described in inventories. Frequently they are all lumped together with decedent's money – his 'purse and apparel' – without any detailed description. One particularly frustrating entry is found in the inventory of George Bowden of Bowden (Cheshire) in 1625: 'all his aparell and all his ridinge furnituer one crosbowe 6 boultes' all valued together at £5. It is rare to get the detail provided by Ellen Wood's Bowden inventory of 1669: 'in Coates and wastcoates' 11s 6d; 'in shoes and stockinges' 4s 6d; 'one seardge hood' 1s 6d; 'linen Cloathes £1; gloves 6d; 'one hatt' 4d; 'one gowne' 7s. More information about clothing can sometimes be found in wills, as has already been noted. The appraisers of Margaret Harrys, widow, of Calthorpe (Oxfordshire), gave a longer description of her clothing than is usual: 'her apparell' consisted of 'two gownes, too petticottes, one hate, smockes, hose, shooes and lynnnen'. Her will, however, went into greater detail, with the clothes divided amongst six different legatees. These clothes, incidentally, would not have been included in her husband's inventory: they were *bona paraphernalia*, her own personal property.

The frequent lumping together of cash and clothing emphasizes the fact that cash was frequently scarce. If people had money to spare, it was likely to be lent rather than stashed under the bed. It has been estimated that some forty per cent of inventories in eastern England record debts due to the deceased. In early seventeenth-century Darlington, only a handful of decedents can be identified who were not participating in the credit network at the time of their death. The great majority of people regularly lent and/or borrowed money. Inventories generally record the names of debtors, although this sometimes depended on the practice of the local court. In Lichfield Diocese, for example, it was not the practice to itemize debts owing to the deceased.

Debts were problematic for executors. If they were secured by a bond, then they could be recovered in a court of law, and are therefore likely to be recorded in inventories. The debts recorded in shop books were generally not secured by bond, but their importance was recognized by statute in 1609. They could be retrievable if action was taken within twelve months of the date they were entered. If there was neither bond nor shop book, then debts could be irretrievable. One contemporary commentator argued that such debts should only be recorded in inventories if they had been recovered. In practice, however, many 'desperate debts' were recorded. Accounts, where they are available, should show whether they were in fact recovered.

Leases present a different type of problem. Leases for lives were regarded as a form of real estate until 1676, when they became available to executors and administrators to settle debt. From 1741 they were treated as personal estate. A lease for years, by contrast, had always been treated as a part of the personal estate, and should have been included in inventories. There were many grey areas. In the South West, where leases for three lives or ninety-nine years were common, they were always included in inventories. The 'dwelling hous' of Robert Coles of Willand (Devon) was valued at £40 in 1671; it was presumably held on a lease.

Fixtures posed another difficulty. A house was real property, and consequently of no interest to appraisers. The concept of the heirloom, according to Burn's *Ecclesiastical law* (1763, pp. 303–4), laid down that goods 'that by custom have gone with the house', such as grates, firebacks, hangings, and so on, should be treated as real property and excluded from inventories. E.G. Jacob's *New law dictionary* (5th ed., 1744) argued that all large household implements were heirlooms. However, the medieval house had few fixtures, and medieval lawyers regarded items such as window glass, wainscoting, and internal doors, which were innovations in their day, as removable, and therefore as personal estate. Robert Hill of Clophill (Bedfordshire) had 'ye glasse of all ye windowes' valued at 10s in 1619. In Gloucestershire, window glass disappeared from inventories after 1660. It came to be regarded as permanent fittings, rather than as removable. By contrast, a Bicester (Oxfordshire) inventory of 1615 shows what could happen after the taking of an inventory. It refers to 'on loft over the Halle to be taken up and unnayled'. Small scale industrial equipment such as anvils, cyder presses, and spinning machines were treated similarly. Such goods grew in size during the early modern period. Frequently they clearly became immoveable, and thus part of the real estate. The fact that they do not appear in a particular inventory does not mean that they were not present. It was, of course, in the interests of creditors and legatees to treat them as personal estate. Many lawsuits were fought over such issues. The pressure of litigation in the eighteenth century, and the clear injustice of depriving creditors and legatees of any claim on so-called heirlooms, helped to modify strict interpretations of the law on this point.

The distinction between real and personal estate was also difficult to draw in relation to the fruits of the earth. Medieval lawyers laid down that the natural produce of the earth was real estate, while produce that was the result of human effort was personal estate. Hence growing grass was not included in inventories, but hay that had been cut was. Crops that had to be cut, such as standing wheat, were regarded as personal estate, and were the responsibility of the executor. Those that had to be dug, such as potatoes and carrots, were real estate, and belonged to the heir. These distinctions were not always apparent to appraisers, and many divergences from the rule may be found.

Some livestock were also excluded. Rabbits, fish, deer, and doves, amongst others, were not regarded as domesticated, and were therefore not listed in inventories.

There are two further omissions from probate inventories that are important. Most people participated in the early modern credit market, as both creditors and debtors. Inventories record the debts due to decedents, but (usually) not the debts that they owed. Secondly, inventories have nothing to say about income, which is a prime determinant of wealth. The total value of an inventory therefore does not necessarily reflect the wealth of the deceased, and any study of the wealth recorded in them must take this into account.

Probate accounts, where they survive, can solve one of these problems, since they record the payment of debts owed, and can consequently give a fuller picture. It is much more difficult to calculate income.

A wide range of other topics may be dealt with in inventories. Sometimes these are actually nothing to do with probate. For example, the inventory of Isabel Humble of Stannington (Northumberland) records that

> as for James Humble of Shotton, what filial portion was left him was spent and more on him for seeking cure for the [Kings] evill and after his return from London was Lame to his death.

Scrofula was thought to be curable by the king's touch. James (who was presumably Isabel's son) had been to London to seek his cure, but had evidently failed. Another example is provided by the inventory of Mary Yates of Madeley (Shropshire), which reveals that she was 'murthered by one George Jenkes and others' in 1687.

Probate inventories provide information relating to a wide range of people and topics, according to a set of rules that was applied reasonably consistently. Consequently, they can easily be compared with each other, and it is possible to derive statistics from them, provided that their various biases and exclusions are allowed for. Inventories enable us to trace the way in which goods such as beds and bedding, tables and chairs, cups and saucers, knives and forks, became ubiquitous. They reveal that the quantity of goods found in Englishmen's homes increased dramatically between 1500 and 1800. That increase itself caused the format of inventories to change, and perhaps had something to do with the fact that they ceased to be compiled. In the sixteenth century, inventories were simply lists of goods. In the seventeenth century, they tended to list goods room by room, so that we can see how particular rooms were used. By the eighteenth century, there were so many goods to list that appraisers gave up. They simply valued all the goods in one room together, without describing them in detail.

Chapter 5

WHAT CAN I FIND IN OTHER PROBATE RECORDS?

Animals have these advantages over man: they never hear the clock strike, they die without any idea of death, they have no theologians to instruct them, their last moments are not disturbed by unwelcome and unpleasant ceremonies, their funerals cost them nothing, and no one starts lawsuits over their wills.

Voltaire

Litigation

Lawsuits concerning probate were one of the commonest types of litigation heard by ecclesiastical courts. Disputes centered around two matters. The authenticity of the will could be challenged, and rival claimants to the administration could make their case. Nuncupative wills and codicils were particularly open to challenge. Depositions in such cases frequently describe the process of will-making. Secondly, interested parties could question the way in which an estate was being administered. Legatees whose legacies had not been paid could demand payment. An executor who had commenced the administration of an estate without obtaining a grant of probate could be challenged. Inventories and accounts might be demanded or questioned. Johana Muttacott, brought before the archdeaconry court of Barnstaple in 1578, deposed that

> she ded not procure nor cause to be procured Any Administracon out of the prerogative Courte nor none was procured by her consente nor by her procurement as she belyveth.

She then went on to list all the goods that should have been included in her husband's inventory. She had obviously not bothered to obtain a grant of probate, and had been challenged.

Executors could also be challenged for political or religious motives. Arthur Edgeley of Smeatonwood (Cheshire) had been appointed executor in his brother Richard's nuncupative will in 1653, and made the guardian of his nephew. After the Restoration of Charles II in 1660, the will was challenged, and, in one of the interrogatories, witnesses were asked,

> hath he [Arthur] bene conformable to the Church Discipline Or otherwise Schismatically affected and hath he not perversely practiced and Lied & Ruled and done against the King the Church and his Neighbours in many things and is he not for such a notoriously accompted reputed and taken and therefore unfit to take Care and Educacon of Children.

One witness responded by accusing Arthur of having been a sequestrator 'in the late time of troubles', that is, he had been responsible for seizing Royalists' goods on behalf of Parliament. Unfortunately, we do not know the verdict of the court.

When there was doubt, wills could be proved 'in solemn form'. This process required all those with an interest in a will to be cited to attend a hearing. Witnesses were cross-examined on the circumstances in which the will was made. The court deliberated and produced a final 'sentence' on the case. This procedure gave the executor much greater security: the court's verdict could only be challenged in a superior court. That explains why the executor of Thomas Gray of Newhall (Cheshire) went to court in early 1641. He had entrusted Gray's will to the local incumbent, Randle Harding, so that he could secure a commission to take the necessary oath. Harding deposed that

> soe soone as hee came into the house, [he did] looke for the said will in his pockett where hee did verily beleeve hee had put the same, but could not find it, & there was the first place that he missed the same & perceaved that he had lost it.

The will was subsequently found and proved, but not before several witnesses had had to answer no fewer than twenty-two interrogatories to satisfy the court that the newly-found will was in fact the genuine lost will.

Some matters had to be dealt with in secular courts such as King's Bench and Chancery. The descent of real property was subject to their jurisdiction; consequently, suitors who sought to challenge the devise of land in wills used the secular courts. Similarly, dissatisfied creditors could sue executors for payment of their debts – although the non-payment of tithes was a matter for the church courts.

Much of the information contained in allegations, interrogatories, and depositions related to family feuds and arguments. Remarriage frequently aroused suspicion, especially when minor children were involved. Records of testamentary litigation may be particularly useful in tracing widows whose second marriages led to disputes.

Litigation was commenced by the issue of a citation, initiated by the plaintiff, which summoned the defendant to court. The plaintiff would then issue an allegation, accompanied by interrogatories, that is, written questions to witnesses. The sworn answers of witnesses testifying to the genuineness or otherwise of the will would be written down. Sometimes the plaintiff issued further replications, which witnesses had to answer. All this evidence would be in writing, and presented to the judge in open court. He would hear the arguments of proctors on both sides, and make his judgement, known as a sentence. In the Diocese of Lichfield, many of the defendants were widows, who had frequently remarried, and who had perhaps been slow to wind up the affairs of their first husbands. The allegations made against them, the interrogatories issued by complainants, the written depositions of witnesses, and the sentences of judges, contain a huge mass of social history that is likely to yield much of interest to both family and local historians. Depositions are particularly interesting. There may also be exhibits produced in court, such as copies of wills (sometimes bogus), inventories, certificates of burials from parish registers, newspaper advertisements, and even bibles. Most of these documents are in English; however, formal records of proceedings are in Latin before 1733 (except for the period 1651–60). It was possible to launch a legal challenge against a will for up to thirty years after it was proved, so it may be worth searching for evidence of litigation over a period of several decades. The evidence is not particularly common, but nor is it rare; in Bowden (Cheshire), there is evidence of litigation for one in every twenty-one decedents recorded in the probate court.

Appeals from archdeaconry courts lay to the bishop's Consistory, whose records are in local record offices; appeals from Consistories lay to PCC whose records are in TNA, or to the Court of Arches. Appeals from peculiar jurisdictions went to Arches. Arches records are held at Lambeth Palace Library, and are available in a microfiche collection, widely available in libraries:

- *Records of the Court of Arches 1554–1911*. Microfiche. Chadwyck-Healey, *c.*1983. This is indexed in Houston, J. *Index of cases in the records of the Court of Arches at Lambeth Palace Library 1660–1912*. Index Library 85. British Record Society, 1972.

Appeal from the PCC lay to the High Court of Delegates, whose records are in TNA, class DEL1-11. A detailed listing of PCC records of litigation can be found in Chapter 8 of Grannum & Taylor's *Wills & probate records* (see below, p. 108). Records of PCY are held by the Borthwick Institute. Over 2,700 testamentary causes from York are indexed in:

- Cause papers in the Diocesan Courts of the Archbishopric of York
  www.hrionline.ac.uk/causepapers

The records of equity and common law courts are preserved in TNA. A number of 'research guides' can be found on its webpage **www.national archives.gov.uk/records/research-guide-listing.htm**. Some 26,000 disputes over inheritance in the Court of Chancery are indexed in:

- Inheritance Disputes Index 1574–1714
  www.britishorigins.com/help/aboutbo-indis.aspx

The court of King's Bench in session, by Thomas Rowlandson (c.1808). (From Wikimedia Commons)

Act Books

The grant of probate, or of letters of administration, was usually (although not always) recorded in act books, or registers of administrations granted. These are likely to be in date order; they will give the date of the grant, the name, status, and parish of the deceased, the name of the executor or administrator, the date(s) by which an inventory and/or account had to be exhibited, and whether a bond had been entered into. Additional information may also be provided, for example, the deceased's place of death, his marital status, the name of the commissioner who swore the executor, and the value of the estate. Act books are likely to be in Latin prior to 1733 (except for the period 1651–60). Sometimes, they are internally indexed. If a will, inventory, or administration bond survives, it is unlikely that the act book will provide any useful additional information. However, if these are not available, it may be worth checking.

Commissions

Administration was only granted when the administrator had sworn an oath to do his duty properly. Local clergymen were sometimes commissioned to take this oath; the issuance of their commissions may have been separately recorded in a commission book. These give the name of the deceased, the commissioner, and the executor to be sworn. They may include useful details. Records of oaths sworn sometimes also survive attached to wills, as can be seen below.

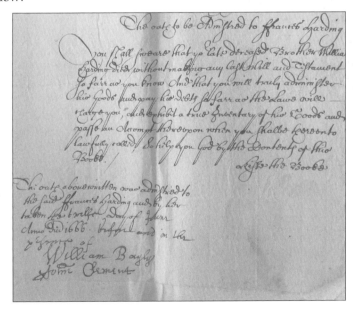

The oath taken by Francis Harding of Stourton, Wiltshire, before Commissioners, 1665. (Wiltshire & Swindon Archives P2/H/634)

Administration Bonds

Administration bonds were frequently – in some archives, usually – attached to wills and inventories. They were required by an Act of 1670, but had been common from around 1600. Bonds had a standard wording, which was formalized by the same Act. Until 1733, bonds were partly in English, partly in Latin. An example is given below. Printed forms such as the one

A typical administration bond. James and Mary Lang of Week St Mary, 1629. (Cornwall Record Office AP/L/325)

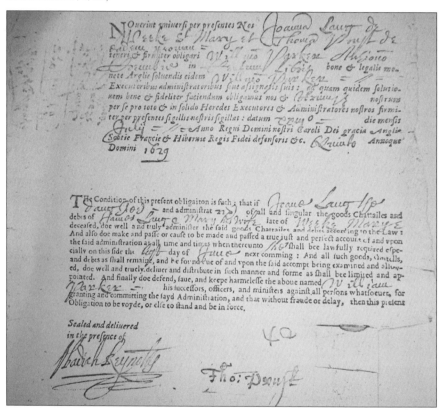

Translation of Latin:
Know all men by these presents that We, Joanna Lang of Week St Mary, & Thomas Proust of the same, yeoman, are held and firmly bound to William Parker, Archdeacon of Cornwall, in £100 of good and lawful money of England, to be paid to him the said William Parker his executors, administrators or assigns. For the good and faithful payment of which sum we bind ourselves, and each of us for the whole and our heirs executors and administrators firmly by these presents sealed with our seals. Dated 23rd July in the 5th year of our Lord Charles by the Grace of God King of England Scotland, France and Ireland, defender of the Faith, etc, Anno Domini 1629.

illustrated were frequently used. Bonds required administrators, and sometimes executors, to produce an inventory, or perhaps an account, under a monetary penalty for failure to do so – perhaps double the estimated value of the estate. Sometimes they also imposed other obligations, for example, the obligation to ensure that minors were educated. Bonds named administrators and their sureties, and gave their residences and sometimes their occupations. It is worth noting these details, and trying to trace any relationships of both the administrator and the sureties to the deceased. Their signatures and/or marks can also be used to study literacy.

Probate Accounts

Wills record how the testator intended his property to be distributed. If, however, you wish to know how the property actually was distributed, you must refer to the probate account. Accounts were submitted to the court by executors and administrators (although they were frequently actually written by court officials) in order to secure release from the obligations of their office. It is probable that they were only prepared when the courts specifically demanded them, as comparatively few survive. They date mainly from the period c.1580 to c.1685. The majority relate to intestate estates. In the Diocese of Lichfield, the numbers increased slightly following the Act of 1670, which required the date by which accounts had to be submitted to be noted in the administration bond. The increase did not last. Another Act, in 1685, laid down that courts could require an account only in cases where the rights of minors or creditors were affected, or if the next of kin demanded one. This Act led directly to a very sharp fall in the number of accounts exhibited in the courts. It also led to a change in the character of accounts, whose format (at least in Lichfield Diocese) varied considerably. Their focus would be on the point at issue between the parties – perhaps the cost of bringing up young children, or the number of debts.

Some accounts were submitted within a few weeks of the grant of probate. The process of administering an estate could, however, take a long time, especially if there were young children. The accountant of Richard Smalbone of Steventon (Berkshire) spent over fifteen years administering his estate, and paid out £85 5s 'for the bord schooling appareling and bringing vp of Thomas Smalbone sonne of the sayd Richard', between June 1567 and Christmas 1582. Once the court had accepted an account, and the 'quietus est' had been recorded, the task of the accountant was at an end. But some accounts took many years.

Accounts open by rehearsing the names of the deceased and the accountant (the executor or administrator), together with details of their residences and occupations. Any relationship between them may be noted. They are not always explicitly dated, but may be endorsed with the date on which they were exhibited in court.

Accounts show the 'charge' or 'onus' and the 'discharge' or 'exoneratio'. The charge is usually formulaic, and simply gives the total value of the inventory, with any adjustments that were necessary for incorrect valuation, or for changes caused by the passing of time. For example, rents due to the estate might fall due before the account was prepared; desperate debts thought unrecoverable by appraisers might be recovered by the accountant; the auction of goods might yield more than the appraisers anticipated. For example, in 1682 Maurice Greenfield's Sussex accountant sold his goods for £42 more than the appraisers had estimated. Prices recorded for goods in probate accounts record the actual amounts received (or paid), rather than an appraisers' estimate of what they were worth.

The discharge lists expenditure incurred in administering the estate. Expenditure could cover a wide range. The first call on the estate, after 1687, was any fine imposed for refusal to be buried in wool. Any moneys due to the overseers then had to be paid, followed by funeral expenses, and the costs associated with probate. After these expenses had been met, the debts of the deceased had to be paid before legacies could be distributed.

Every accountant had to meet the cost of a funeral. The probate account for William Dore, labourer, of Reading in 1635 has many entries relating to payments made. The parish clerk received 10s 'for towleing the bell and making of the deceaseds graue'; the coffin cost 13s 4d; £1 was paid to the officiating minister; 'Cakes and beere & other prouision at his funerall' cost £1 10s; a further 16s was laid out 'for Ribbonds & points', and the shroud and 'woemen which layd him out' cost 15s.

More expense was incurred in the process of probate. Scribes and appraisers had to be paid; so did fees at the probate court. In 1667, the accountant of Thomas Tegge, innholder of Pangbourne (Berkshire) had to pay out 12s 6d 'for the Letters of the Administracion, obligacion vpon the same, ingrossing of the Inventries and Apparitors fee', 2s 6d 'for ingrossing of the Inventaries', 6s 8d 'for conceaving of this account in writing and Counsell about the same', 10s 'for the decree of the Judge in examining of this accompt, 3s 4d 'for ingrossing of this Accompt', and 10s 'for the quietus est'.

Once these costs had been met, the debts owed by the deceased could be paid. Probate accounts provide more information concerning the credit network of early modern England than any other documents. They reveal the extent to which an administrator could recover debts due to the deceased, and the extent to which the debts of the deceased could not be paid. Most people owed money; accounts show how these debts were paid off. John Stinchcombe of Frampton Cotterell (Gloucestershire), for example, owed £6 on a bond to Thomas Jarvis of Winterbourne, and had another debt of

The bier in Dinton Church (Wiltshire), used for parish funerals. Any charges for using it would have been recorded in probate accounts (and also in churchwardens' accounts).

£1 owed to Ann Bradstone of Thornbury when he died in 1628. These were paid off by his accountant. Stinchcombe was a labourer, whose inventory totalled a mere £33 17s 2d.

Accountants also had to collect debts due to the deceased. This was not necessarily an easy task. The accountant of William Webb, mercer, of Newbury (Berkshire) had to pay no less than 26s 8d for

> copyeng out the debts mentioned in the sayd deceased his shop booke, all which or the most part of them ar very doubtfull and despeerate and therefore not putt into the inventory.

The debts of the deceased frequently included the cost of 'physick', that is, medical expenses, incurred during the decedent's final illness, which had to be paid. The accountant of John Rose of South Morton (Berkshire) recorded 12s 'payd to 'Dr Curtois for physick' in 1695. A vivid description of the consequences of plague can be inferred from the 1610 account of Thomas Smalebone of Bucklebury (Berkshire). His house had to be shut up after his death, to prevent the spread of the disease. Surviving members of his household were incarcerated for ten months; his accountant had to pay 'for provision into the house' on many occasions.

The act of dying itself incurred costs. Manorial lords were frequently entitled to a heriot – often the best beast – on the death of a tenant. The accountant of Anne Eldridge of Colsey (Berkshire) had to pay the bailiff of 'my Lord of Holland' £7 15s for four heriots. Parochial clergymen were also entitled to a customary payment on the death of a parishioner. When John Justice of Pangbourne (Berkshire) died in 1668, his accountant paid 10s 'to Mr Ambrose Stavelin for a Mortuarie due to him from the deceased'. In the case of accidental death, the cause of death – the deodand – might be forfeit to the Crown. In 1629, the accountant of Thomas Strange of Charney (Berkshire) recorded the surrender of a deodand – his horse – which had evidently been the cause of his death. She also had to pay the coroner, Mr Thomas Head, 6s 9d as his fee for conducting an inquest.

The accountant's own costs, such as travel to attend court, had to be met. Tegge's widow charged his estate with 12s for 'the charges of this accomptant hir sureties in coming to Oxford to obtaine the letters of Administration & for the hire of horses and horsemeat'.

The administration of an estate might also incur costs. The expenses of an estate did not cease with the death of its owner. Wages of servants and labourers had to be paid, landlords still expected their rents until tenancies expired, taxes were levied, crops had to be harvested, animals had to be tended. The accountant of Elizabeth Bayly of Winterbourne (Gloucestershire) in 1677 'paid Mr Hugh Browne for rent' £7 10s, 'paid to severall workemen for worke done to the house at Morend' £8 10s 2d, and 'paid his brother Thomas for worke done by his plough and money laid out by him' £11 15s.

If there were young children, the cost of their education and maintenance had to be included in accounts. Food, clothing, apprenticeship, and shelter all cost money. The administrator of Rowland Hughes, who died at Banbury in 1611, had to meet various costs associated with his son John's apprenticeship:

> for byndyng of John Hewes an apprentice at London to one Mr William Allostronge £10; whereof receaved againe when he runned away from his M^r £4.

John evidently gave his guardians some trouble. They had to pay several different people for his board, and also had to enter a second apprenticeship indenture after he had run away from his first master. One wonders if he was related to any of the people whom he lodged with.

The upheavals of the Civil War sometimes imposed much greater costs (and worry) on accountants. In 1645, Mary Godfrey of Cumnor (Berkshire), acting as accountant for her husband, had lost two horses, and one cow, together worth £7, seized by 'the Parliament forces'. She also had to pay 12s 'for redeeming the rest of hir cattell'. To add insult to injury, the Parliamentarians also stole 'the apparrell of the deceased', worth £2. This was all in addition to the various sums of 'contribution money' and other exactions she had to pay to the garrisons at Abingdon, Farringdon, and Oxford. Yet more: a 'load of straw carried into Abingdon garrison' cost her 3s 2d; 'the heyre of a Teame to the kinges Armie' required expenditure of a further 3s 2d. All of these losses were recorded in the probate account.

The third element in an account is the allocation, usually in Latin. This either notes that expenditure had exceeded the value of the estate, or sets out who is to receive any remaining money. This was determined either by the will, or, in the case of intestates, by the 1670 Act for the better settling of intestate estates. The allocation is followed by the 'quietus est', acquitting the accountant of any further liability in respect of the estate. Accounts are likely to close with the signature of a court official, and perhaps of the accountant.

Much of the information provided by probate accounts would have gone unrecorded if they had not been written. The account for John Stinchcombe has already been mentioned; it identified his servant, his creditors, and his landlord, none of whom are mentioned in his inventory. He was a mere labourer. The accounts of wealthier decedents sometimes reveal much more information. The inventory of John Eaton of Bowdon (Cheshire) totalled £229 8s 5d. Neither it nor his will have been found; however, his account lists no fewer than thirty-three payments made to legatees. It also records payments made for thatching, shearing, cutting hay, winnowing and 'leading' corn, mending a cart saddle, 'smithy worke', and a wide range of other tasks undertaken by tradesmen and labourers. Apothecaries' bills, tithes, the wages of servants, and debts due, all had to be paid, together with, not least, 'funerality expens' amounting to £22.

Sometimes it is possible to deduce religious beliefs from accounts. For example, Edward Crayforde, who died in Kent in 1558, had a distinctly Catholic funeral; his accountant had to pay 'three priests and ii clarks for Celebratinge masses and seyinge of Dyrrigs iiis viiid'. Other accounts may help us to trace the impact of plague. The shutting up of infected households, and the nursing and medical care required for plague victims, both had to be paid for.

The range of topics covered can also be illustrated by the 1690 account of William Hume, who had been the keeper of Durham gaol. His executors had to pay £5 for keeping the gaol for thirty weeks, under a bond which Hume had entered when he accepted the position. Sadly, the amount of detail in probate accounts given does vary, and is not always as extensive; in the Diocese of Lichfield, for example, the names of creditors are frequently not stated.

Once expenses had been paid, the balance remaining had to be distributed amongst the legatees. If the will is missing, this portion of the account can act as a substitute. If, however, there was not sufficient money in the estate to meet legacies, that will be revealed in the payments made. In the Province of York, as already noted, testators only controlled the distribution of a third of their estates until 1692. Probate accounts from the Province reflect that fact.

If there were no will, the distribution of the remainder of the estate after expenses was governed by customary law, or, after 1670, by the Statute of Distribution. This laid down that a third of the estate was to be given to the widow, and the remainder divided equally between children. This division is likely to be reflected in the accounts of intestates.

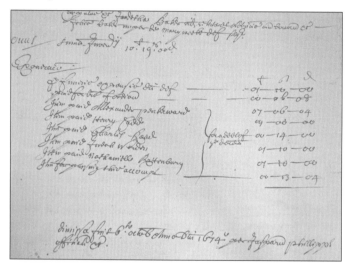

Account of Judith Baker, widow of John Baker of Week St Mary, Cornwall, 1674.
(Cornwall Record Office AP/B/1673)

Transcript (with Latin translated):
Account of Judith Baker, widow, relict and administrator of the goods and chattels of John Baker, late of Week St Mary, deceased

Onus   Inventory total 10^l 19^s 00^d

Exoneratio

		L s d
For funeral expenses of the said deceased		01-10-00
paid for lrs of adion[1]		00-06-08
Itm paid Allexander Penkerward	for a debt of ye decd	07-06-04
Itm paid Henry Cadd	[ditto]	04-00-00
Itm paid Charles Read	[ditto]	00-14-00
Itm paid Judah Wordon	[ditto]	01-10-00
Itm paid Nathaniell Rattenbury	[ditto]	01-10-00
Itm paid for passing this account		00-13-04

Was dismissed 6th October 1674 by Jaspar Philipps, official[2].

---

1. Letters of administration.
2. The total spent was not calculated; it was actually £17 10s 4d, i.e. more than the inventory total.

Accountants were supposed to exhibit acquittances or cancelled bonds for any payment out of the estate amounting to over £2. Such documents can sometimes be found attached to their accounts.

Accounts give a much fuller picture than inventories alone, and enable us to reach much more accurate conclusions about wealth. They are also a useful source for the history of credit and of medicine, and for the culture of death. Unfortunately, their survival rate is poor. Perhaps one in twenty wills has an attached probate account. After 1685, they only survive if the distribution of the estate was challenged.

Chapter 6

WHERE AND HOW CAN I FIND PROBATE RECORDS?

Indexes and Catalogues

The first task facing the probate researcher is to discover where his ancestors' wills were proved, or where administrations were granted. Before 1858, most wills were proved in ecclesiastical courts. There were several hundred different courts. Their records were not always well kept, as Charles Dickens complained in *David Copperfield*:

> I replied ... that perhaps it was a little nonsensical that the Registry of the Court, containing the original wills of all persons leaving effects within the immense province of Canterbury, for three whole centuries, should be an accidental building, never designed for the purpose, leased by the registrars for their own private emolument, unsafe, not even ascertained to be fire-proof, choked with the important documents it held, and positively, from the roof to the basement, a mercenary speculation of the registrars, who took great fees from the public, and crammed the public's wills away anyhow and anywhere, having no other object than to get rid of them cheaply.

The conditions in which probate records are now stored are a vast improvement on those which Dickens experienced. The PCC's archives are housed in modern, purpose-built accommodation at Kew. There is no central repository for the records of other courts; they are scattered in numerous different record offices – but they are looked after properly. Probate courts are listed in Appendix 1, together with the location of their archives. It is necessary to be aware of the range of courts that could grant probate. The searcher for wills in Kings Langley (Hertfordshire) would have to consult the archives of the Archdeaconry of Huntingdon (which are in two different record offices), the Consistory Court of Lincoln, and the PCC. Unless, that is, he consulted the bibliography below, and discovered that there is a printed edition!

All probate courts kept separate registers of the wills they proved and administrations they granted. Most (not all) wills are indexed. Some of these

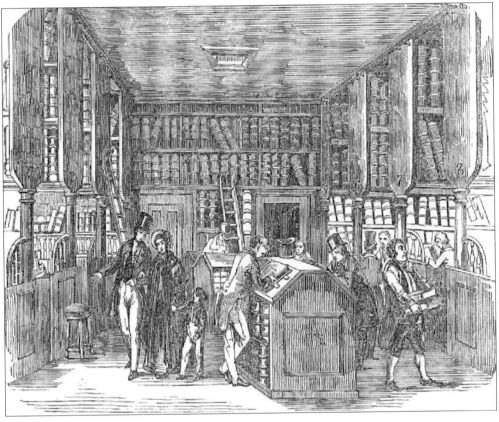

Searching for PCC wills at Doctors' Commons in the nineteenth century.

indexes are available on the internet; others are in book format; yet others are unpublished. There is no comprehensive overall index. It may be necessary to consult several different indexes to find the will of a particular testator.

A project is currently in progress to digitize and merge many of these will indexes. The new database is being hosted by Origins Network on a pay-per-view basis. Initially, it will include many of the indexes published by the British Record Society in its *Index Library* series. A number of will indexes from other sources, such as the Borthwick Institute in York, are also being included. Ultimately, it is planned to digitize at least some of the original wills; however, none are online at the time of writing. By the time you read this, the project will be more advanced. For details of the information currently available, visit:

- National Wills Index **www.nationalwillsindex.com**

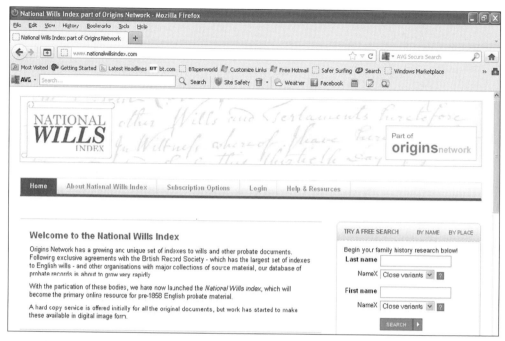

The National Wills Index.

It is likely to be some years – if ever – before the aims of the National Wills Index are fully met. Until then, it is necessary to use a range of other indexes. Many are online. For a fairly full listing of the latter, consult:

- Your Archives: Online Probate Indexes **http://yourarchives.national archives.gov.uk/index.php?title=Online_Probate_Indexes**

Much information about probate records can be found on the websites of the record offices which hold them. Their online catalogues frequently include indexes to wills held in the archives of probate courts. They also include entries relating to wills found amongst family and estate papers, and elsewhere. Catalogues are, however, rarely complete. Few record offices have managed to index all their holdings. If you are unable to find the documents you seek, you should always ask record office staff for advice on unindexed material. Record office websites are listed at:

- Archon Directory **www.nationalarchives.gov.uk/archon**

Many record offices have contributed portions of their catalogue to union catalogues. These portions are not necessarily identical to those hosted by the record offices themselves. Both should be consulted. The major union catalogues are:

- A2A: Access to Archives
  www.nationalarchives.gov.uk/a2a
  Indexes the holdings of over 400 record offices

- Archives Hub
  www.archiveshub.ac.uk
  Union catalogue for university and college archives

- Aim 25: Archives in London and the M25 Are
  www.aim25.ac.uk

It has already been pointed out that few record office catalogues are complete. Union catalogues are even less complete. A2A, for example, estimates that only thirty per cent of the archives held by participants are listed in its database.

The result of a search for 'Probate' on Archives Hub, showing the important collection of probate records from York Diocesan Archive at the top of the list.

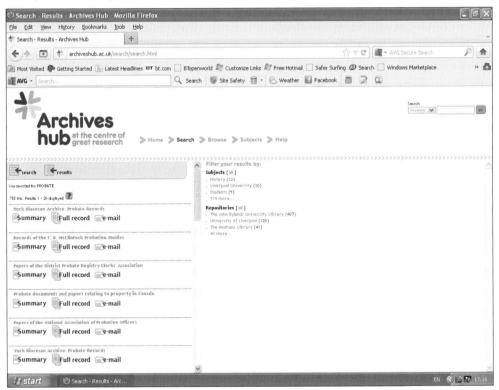

Many indexes were compiled before the internet revolution. Some of these were published; others were not. For details of these indexes, together with more information about particular probate courts, consult:

- Gibson, Jeremy, & Churchill, Else. *Probate jurisdictions: where to look for wills*. 5th ed., Federation of Family History Societies, 2002.

This volume is updated by:

- Andrew Millard's Genealogy: Recent Indexes to English, Welsh, Scottish and Irish Probate Records
  www.dur.ac.uk/a.r.millard/genealogy/probate.php

It has already been pointed out that indexes in the British Record Society's *Index Library* series form a major proportion of the National Wills Index database. These indexes can also be consulted in hard copy in numerous libraries and record offices. Some of them may also be found on e-book sites such as the Internet Archive **www.archive.org**. A few are available, pay-per-view, on Ancestry **www.ancestry.co.uk** (click 'card catalog' and 'filter titles' for wills). For a full listing of the volumes available, visit:

- Guide to Record Societies and their Publications (Texts and Calendars)
  www.royalhistoricalsociety.org/textandcalendars.php

For the British Record Society itself, visit:

- British Record Society **www.britishrecordsociety.org**

The holdings of *Index Library* volumes in university and national libraries can be checked by consulting:

- Copac National, Academic, and Specialist Library Catalogue
  http://copac.ac.uk

Useful (but not always reliable) information about indexes to probate records can also be found by searching 'probate' + [county]' at Family Search's:

- England Probate Records
  https://wiki.familysearch.org/en/England_Probate_Records
  Scroll to the 'courts' section of the page and click on specific courts.

Many published and unpublished will indexes are held by the Society of Genealogists. It is worth consulting the catalogue of this collection, even if you are not able to use the Society's library: many of the items listed can also be found in other libraries. See:

- Newington-Irvine, Nicholas, *Will indexes and other probate material in the library of the Society of Genealogists*. Society of Genealogists, 1996.

The National Archives, home to the archive of the PCC. (Courtesy of Chris Reynolds)

Published will indexes are also listed in the county volumes of the present author's *Genealogical Bibliographies* series.

Prerogative Court Archives: Canterbury and York

The archive of the PCC is the most substantial collection of probate records in England and Wales. It is held by TNA. In theory, this court only proved wills where the testator held property in more than one diocese, or where he had died at sea or abroad. In practice, the prestige of the court meant that the wills of many wealthy individuals were proved there. During the interregnum (1649–60), all wills were proved in London, and are filed amongst PCC archives.

The court kept various different series of records. Its will registers (PROB11) form one of these series. These contain copies of most wills proved in the Court between 1384 and 1858. Most, but not all. Executors had to pay to have their wills registered; if they did not pay, their wills were not registered, even though a grant of probate had been made by the court.

Over a million wills were copied into these registers (including all wills proved in England and Wales during the interregnum). They have all been digitized, and are available on TNA's Documents Online database:

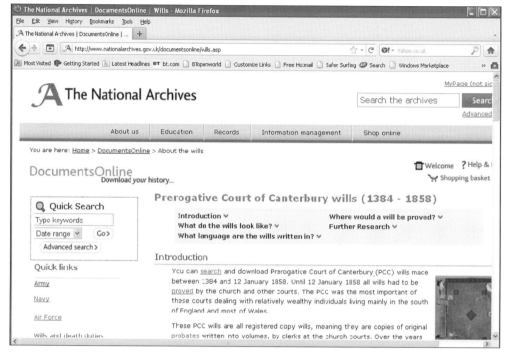

Documents Online PCC webpage.

- Documents Online: Prerogative Court of Canterbury Wills (1384–1858)
  www.nationalarchives.gov.uk/documentsonline/wills.asp

The index to this database is free to view, but there is a fee for downloading images.

The ease of access to PCC registered wills tends to obscure the fact that many other wills and related documents are preserved in the archives of this court. Almost 7,500 original wills, including some that were proved but not registered, are in PROB10. There are four series of supplementary wills, including almost 3,000 rejected by the court (PROB20), a few copies made when wills were removed from the archives for exhibition in another court of law (PROB21), wills lodged with the court for safekeeping (PROB22), and a few copies of post-1782 wills originally proved in lower courts (PROB23). Other PCC probate records related to individuals have not survived as well as wills. Many were lost during the Great Fire of London. Nevertheless, 825 inventories can be found in PROB2 (pre-1601), 5,894 in PROB3 (1701–1782), 26,061 (including some bonds and accounts) in PROB4 (1660–1720), and 6,182 (including related documents) in PROB5 (mostly 1661–1732). Administration bonds can be found in PROB51 (pre-1601), PROB54

(1601–1713), and PROB46 (1714–1858), although these are not yet fully indexed. If the executor was sworn by commission before local clergymen – many were, to avoid the expense of a visit to London – there may be a record of the clergyman's commission in PROB52 or PROB56. Warrants for grants of probate or administration, and for commissions to swear oaths, are in PROB14. Other records include act books (PROB6-9), allegations (PROB18), depositions and answers (PROB24-6), exhibits (PROB31-3 and 35-6), and a variety of other documents. For more information about PCC archives, see:

- Records of the Prerogative Court of Canterbury
  http://discovery.nationalarchives.gov.uk/SearchUI/Details.mvc/Collection/?iAID=236&cref=PROB

In the North, prerogative jurisdiction was exercised by PCY. Like PCC, both the original wills, and registered copies, can be consulted, as can the act books. However, only a few inventories and accounts are available. None of these records are online as yet, although an index to pre-1500 wills is available from Origins Network **www.origins.net/help/aboutNWI-ymed. aspx**. The archives of the PCY, together with those of the courts of Chancery

Searching TNA's catalogue by class number brings up full descriptions of holdings.

and Exchequer for the Diocese of York, and the court of the Dean and Chapter of York, are held by the Borthwick Institute in York. A variety of guides to the Northern Province's probate records are provided at:

- Borthwick Institute for Archives: Research Guides
  www.york.ac.uk/library/borthwick/research-support/research-guides/
- Borthwick Institute: Probate Records **www.york.ac.uk/media/library/ documents/borthwick/3.1.1.20guideprob.pdf**

Other Probate Courts

The archives of the prerogative courts are replicated on a smaller scale by the archives of many other probate courts. Surviving wills proved in these courts, taken together, probably outnumber those proved in the prerogative courts. They should therefore be explored, bearing in mind that wills are not the only probate records likely to contain valuable information about our ancestors, and it is a mistake to limit research to them alone. Many

The Wiltshire Wills Project webpage. (www.wiltshirewills.org)

Wiltshire and Swindon History Centre.

record office websites have pages describing their own collections of probate records. See, for example:

- Devon County Council: Family History: Wills and Probate Records **www.devon.gov.uk/wills_records.htm**
- Lincolnshire County Council: Wills, Administrations and Inventories **www.lincolnshire.gov.uk/residents/archives/collections/guides-to-sources/wills-administrations-and-inventories**

Digitization

In time, it is to be expected that many of the difficulties of finding and using wills will be solved by the use of digital technology. It is much easier to find and use documents which have been digitized, and are online. A number of digitized collections of wills are either currently available, or likely to become so in the next few years. TNA's Documents Online database has already been mentioned. So have the digitization plans of the National Wills Index. Databases for Scotland and Northern Ireland will be discussed in Chapter 9. Other collections include:

- London Signatures **http://search.lma.gov.uk/opac_lma/onlineresources.html**

Scroll down and click title. This includes 10,000 wills from the court of the Archdeaconry of Middlesex.

- Durham and Northumberland Probate Records **http://familyrecords.dur.ac.uk/nei/**

This website includes a valuable introduction to probate records.

81

The National Library of Wales – home of most Welsh wills.

- Wiltshire and Swindon Archive Catalogue – Wiltshire Wills
  www.wiltshirewills.org
- National Library of Wales: Wills and Probate Records
  www.llgc.org.uk/index.php?id=487

Search Strategies

If you cannot find a will amongst the registered wills in a particular court, there are a number of ways in which you can extend your search. You could begin by looking for the original will, rather than the registered copy. That depends on whether the court retained originals (as the PCC did). Probate courts required payment for registering wills, and not all executors were willing to pay.

If this produces no result, check the court's act book to see if a grant of probate was actually made. This may also reveal a grant of administration made if a decedent died without making a will. Unfortunately, checking may be a tedious process, as act books are generally not well indexed (although some indexes to PCC and other administrations have been published in the British Record Society's *Index Library*). You could also check variant spellings of the surname: no spelling was set in stone, and they did vary over the years, e.g. Smith or Smythe. After 1796, most wills can be traced through the Death Duty registers discussed in Chapter 9. Some of the other sources discussed in this chapter may also prove fruitful.

Do not confine your search to the holdings of one particular court. Although the prerogative courts were in theory reserved for those with property in two dioceses, and the Consistory courts were similarly reserved for those with property in two archdeaconries, in practice there was a great deal more flexibility than these rules suggest. The wills of gentry and clergy were frequently proved in the more prestigious Consistory and Prerogative courts, rather than in the humble archdeaconry courts. Peculiar courts also attracted much probate business. Check the records of all the courts which were active in your area of interest – and bear in mind that the will should have been proved where the testator had his property, which was not necessarily where he lived.

If no will can be found, you can still search for other probate documents, such as inventories, administration bonds, and accounts. Sometimes these are indexed with wills; sometimes not. Details of those held by PCC are mentioned above. Until recently, the indexes available for probate accounts were poor. This has been rectified by:

- Spufford, Peter et al, Eds., *Index to the probate accounts of England and Wales*, 2 vols. Index Library 112–3. British Record Society, 1999.

Chapter 7

POST-1858 WILLS

The Probate Act 1857 removed probate jurisdiction from the ecclesiastical courts, and created a national Court of Probate for England and Wales, together with (originally) forty district probate registries which proved wills of lower value. The essential features of the system created in 1857 have remained intact ever since, although there have been several reorganizations of the system of courts. Probate procedure was simplified, and the necessity to employ a proctor to appear on behalf of executors was abolished. Executors were able to appear in person; indeed, it became possible to apply for probate through local Inland Revenue offices. Successful application led to a grant of representation. There were three types of grant: probate was granted to executors named in a valid will; letters of administration were granted when the deceased left no will; letters of administration (with will) could be granted to someone other than an executor when there was a valid will. The latter type of grant could be made if the executor declined to act, was abroad, mentally incapable, a minor, or dead. All types of grant gave the same authority to administer the estate.

The new system commenced activity on 12 January 1858, although of course the early grants of probate concerned testators who died in earlier years – and sometimes much earlier years. Probate could be granted either in the Principal Registry in London (in Llandudno during World War Two), or in a district registry. If it was granted in a district registry, that registry kept the original will, made a registered copy, and sent another copy to the Principal Registry. The latter therefore holds originals or copies of all wills and administrations for England and Wales since 1858. They were indexed annually in the *National Probate Calendar*. Originally, there were separate series of indexes for wills and administrations. These were combined from 1870. If the annual indexes are consulted manually, it is necessary to consult both indexes until 1870. Prior to 1992, the indexes were kept in book form (some of which have important manuscript annotations). For 1993–95, they are on microfiche. Since 1996 they have been computerized.

Between 1858 and 1968, the information provided in the index is fairly detailed, and includes:

- the deceased's full name, final address, and sometimes his/her occupation

- executors' and administrators' full names, with their addresses until 1892
- the relationship of the executor or administrator to the deceased, if any. If the executor is described as 'widow and relict' this indicates that she inherited the whole estate
- the date and place of death
- when and where probate or administration was granted
- the marital status of women, with the names of surviving husbands (husbands are not given after 1958)
- the gross value of the estate (rounded up and expressed as 'effects under £1000' until 1881, after which exact figures were given). This excluded real property until after 1898

After 1968, the information in the calendar was reduced to:

- name and address of the deceased
- date and place of death
- date and place of grant of probate or administration
  the value of the estate

If you are searching before 1941, the easiest way to do it is to visit the almost complete (it may be complete by the time you read this) subscription database hosted by Ancestry.com:

- National Probate Calendar 1861–1941 **www.ancestry.co.uk/probate**

The only complete set of the index, held at First Avenue House, 42–9, High Holborn, London, WC1V 6NP, is free for consultation. Indexes for at least the last fifty years are likely to be held by district registries, although their early hard copy indexes may have been deposited with local record offices. The latter may also hold microfiche copies of the index, pre-1942. TNA holds the same fiche. Some district registries have access to a computerized index listing grants since 1920. The Society of Genealogists holds microfilmed indexes to 1930. The Family History Centres of the Latter Day Saints **www.ancestor-search.info/LOC-LDScentres.htm** can obtain microfilmed indexes up to 1957.

If you are visiting a probate registry in person, it is advisable to phone first to make sure that they can provide the information you need. Applications

Entry in the 1886 index for the will of James Raymond.

RAYMOND James.	19 April.	The Will of James Raymond late of Druidston in the Parish of Nolton in the County of Pembroke Farmer who died 31 January 1886 at Druidston was proved at **Carmarthen** by Margaret Raymond of Druidston Widow the Relict the sole Executrix.
Personal Estate £206 10s.		

HOCKEY Parmenas.	22 November. Letters of Administration
Effects under £300.	of the Personal estate and effects of Parmenas Hockey late of 54 Dolphin-street in the Town of Newport in the County of **Monmouth** Baker Grocer and Beer-house Keeper deceased who died 18 March 1867 at 54 Dolphin-street aforesaid were granted at **Llandaff** to Eliza Hockey of 54 Dolphin-street aforesaid Widow the Relict of the said Deceased she having been first sworn.

Entry in the 1867 index for the administration of Parmenas Hockey. Note that at this earlier date the wealth of the deceased is rounded up.

for searches to be made on your behalf must be made by post (not by email or phone) to: Postal Searches and Copies Department, Leeds District Probate Registry, York House, York Place, Leeds, LS1 2BA. There is a fee for this service (which includes a copy of the will if found). State the full name, address, and date of death of the deceased, and enclose the appropriate fee (see the website for the amount). For more details, visit:

- Probate service **www.justice.gov.uk/guidance/courts-and-tribunals/ courts/probate/index.htm**
  This site includes pages on 'Probate records and family history', 'grants of representation', and a directory of 'probate registries'.

Whilst most wills were proved soon after death, this did not always happen. Sometimes, grants of probate were only applied for when they were needed, which could be decades later, for example, after a widow had died and her husband's house had to be sold (which could only be done if there was a grant). If an index entry cannot be found within a year or two of death, it may be necessary to search the indexes over the next few decades.

If you are still unable to find an entry, there may have been no grant of probate. There could be a number of explanations for this. If the value of an estate was small, then it was not necessary to obtain probate. Even if an individual had a substantial income, it may be that it was drawn from capital in which he had only a life interest – and hence nothing to leave at death. A canny individual anxious to avoid death duties may have distributed his estate to his heirs well before his death, and therefore had no need of a will. A grant of probate was only needed to access investments in bank accounts, shares, or other property. If wealth was in the form of cash or moveable property, there may have been no need for a grant of probate. There is also the possibility that probate was not granted until the decedent had been dead for many years. It is always worth checking the death duty registers (see Chapter 9) to see if they provide any additional information.

It is almost always worth applying for a copy of a will if you find a relevant entry in the index. The only exception to this rule is if the executor is defined as the universal legatee. In that case, the will can be summarized as 'all to wife'.

A further search may be necessary if you find the words 'confirmed' or 'sealed' in the index. This may indicate that the will was proved in Ireland or Scotland. In that case, it is unlikely that the Principal Registry will have any more information than is contained in the index. Details should, however, be available in Edinburgh, Dublin, or Belfast. Chapter 8 is devoted to wills proved in these jurisdictions. The term 'sealed' may also apply to wills proved in other parts of the British Empire and Commonwealth. Wills of the British in India can be consulted in the British Library's India Office Collection **www.bl.uk/reshelp/findhelpregion/asia/india/indiaofficerecords familyhistory/familyresearch.html**. (Click 'wills'.)

Sometimes, additional documentation was retained, especially in district registries. If a will mentions other documents, it is worth asking if they are available. Very occasionally, you may come across the words 'former grant cessate' or 'by decree' in the index. This indicates that the will was disputed, and it should be possible to see a copy of the judgement. TNA holds a small sample of papers relating to contentious probate cases in class J121. These are indexed in TNA's online catalogue.

The original wills are now held centrally in Birmingham. Copies are normally made from the registered wills, rather than the originals. Applications for copies can be made in person at First Avenue House, or through district registries and sub-registries. Copies of grants of probate and letters of administration can also be obtained. Most of the information in them is actually in the Calendar, but the originals may sometimes provide additional information. Postal applications for copies must be sent to the address above. If you have searched the Calendar, you should note the deceased's name, the grant type, the issuing registry, and the date of the grant. If a folio number is cited (for grants made at the Principal Registry between 1858 and 1930), you should note that too; this information will speed up the processing of your request.

Registered copies of wills from district registries have been deposited with some local record offices. Wills for 1858–1925 have been filmed by the Mormons. The film reels can be obtained through their Family History Centres. For details, visit:

- Family Search: Principal Probate Registry
  https://wiki.familysearch.org/en/Principal_Probate_Registry

Post-1858 wills do not differ greatly from the wills proved in ecclesiastical courts, although the invocation of the deity, and other religious clauses, are likely to be missing. Many commence with the words 'This is the last

First Avenue House, home of the Principal Probate Registry. (Courtesy of David Hawgood)

will and testament of ...'. The meaning of these words has already been discussed (above, p. 4–5). The phrase has no real significance after 1858. There is perhaps more legalese gobbledegook in post-1858 wills than in those proved before then. Much of this can safely be ignored. Make a note of the important features: that is, names, relationships, details of legacies, and personal comments.

Bequests may be described as 'absolute' or 'conditional'. An absolute bequest confers ownership on the beneficiary immediately. If a condition is spelt out in the will, it has to be met in order for the beneficiary to benefit. For example, a bequest to an adult son might require him to care for his invalid mother. Bequests might also be made in trust, with named trustees. Such bequests could, for example, be used to provide a minor with an inheritance when he or she came of age or married.

Post-1858 wills continue to name executors, usually family members, although increasingly solicitors or others acting in a professional capacity are named. Where a member of the family is named, he or she was frequently also named as residuary legatee; that is, the beneficiary of the estate once all other legacies had been distributed.

It may also be useful to consult grants of probate, especially if they were made a long time after death. Usually they give the addresses, and sometimes the occupations, of executors. They also give their relationships to testators. These details may not appear in wills. Pre-1892 indexes provide most of these details (apart from occupations), but thereafter they do not give addresses. Post-1968 indexes give none of this information.

The fact that a legacy is given in a will does not necessarily mean that the legatee received it. It is worth comparing the total amount of legacies with the value of the estate as shown in the grant of administration. Prior to 1903, it is possible to see how an estate was actually distributed by consulting the death duty registers (see Chapter 9).

The old Oxford Probate Registry.

If a person died intestate, without leaving a will, then the next of kin had to apply for a grant of letters of administration. If the estate was insolvent, then the leading creditor could be appointed as administrator. The estate had to be distributed according to a set formula, which depended on the number and closeness of surviving relatives, and has varied over the years. The rules relating to personal and real estate were different before 1926. The annual *Whitaker's Almanack*, runs of which can be found in reference libraries, gives the rules for each year of publication, and indicates how the estate should have been split amongst heirs. Again, the actual distribution can be seen in the death duty registers.

The most important change in the law since 1857 was the Married Womens' Property Act 1882, which removed the legal disabilities suffered by wives. They could now hold property in their own right, and could also make wills without their husbands' permission. After this date, a search for a wife's will is much more likely to be successful.

Post-1858 wills are unlikely to be of much use to the local historian, since the cost of obtaining access to all the wills from a particular place is too great. Nevertheless, the will calendars themselves provide a basis for research in some areas. Studies of wealth, for example, could be undertaken from the figures given in the calendars. The information provided relating to executors may also be useful.

Chapter 8

PROBATE RECORDS OUTSIDE OF ENGLAND AND WALES: THE CHANNEL ISLANDS, IRELAND, THE ISLE OF MAN, SCOTLAND

Introduction

Probate laws were not uniform throughout the British Isles. Jurisdictions outside of England and Wales operated their own procedures, both before and after the English switch to secular courts in 1858. In a few cases, where a testator had property in both England and Wales, and under another jurisdiction, probate was granted in one jurisdiction, and the will was 're-sealed' in another.

Channel Islands

There were different arrangements for probate on the different islands. Guernsey is the only place in the British Isles still subject to the jurisdiction of an ecclesiastical probate court. The Ecclesiastical Court of the Bailiwick of Guernsey's jurisdiction extends to Alderney, Sark, Herm and Jethou. It has jurisdiction over wills bequeathing personalty only. Its records date from 1660. Wills bequeathing realty have been proved by HM Greffier since 1841. Records of both courts are held by HM Greffier, The Royal Court House, St Peter Port, Guernsey, GY1 2PB.

In Jersey, wills were proved in the court of the Dean of Jersey until 1949, when the Judicial Greffe took over the responsibility. All wills are held by the Jersey Archive **www.jerseyheritage.org/research-centre/jersey-archive**, and indexed for the period 1660–1971 on its website.

Some Channel Island wills have been filmed by the Latter Day Saints' Family History Library. For details, see:

- Family Search: Channel Island Wills
  https://wiki.familysearch.org/en/Channel_Islands_Wills

The Channel Islands were in the Province of Canterbury, so the wills of island testators who held property in England may be in PCC.

Ireland

The Irish system of probate was similar to that which operated in England and Wales. Until 1857, probate was granted by the diocesan courts of the Church of Ireland. Superior jurisdiction was exercised by the Archbishop of Armagh's Prerogative Court, which proved the wills of testators who owned property in more than one diocese.

When probate jurisdiction was transferred to secular courts in 1857, it was discovered that many records were missing. Unfortunately, the decision was taken to centralize the remaining records. They were eventually deposited in the Irish Public Record Office, transcribed into will and grant books, and then indexed. The original probate records, and most of the will and grant books, were destroyed when the building was blown up in 1922.

Surviving Irish pre-1858 Will and Grant Books in the National Archives of Ireland include:

- Prerogative Court will books 1664–84, 1706–8, 1726–8, 1728–9, 1777, 1813, and 1834.
- Prerogative Court grant books 1684–8, 1748–51, and 1839.
- Diocese of Cashel grant books 1840–45.
- Diocese of Connor will books 1818–20 and 1853–58.
- Diocese of Connor grant books 1818–20 and 1853–58.
- Diocese of Down will books 1850–58.
- Diocese of Down grant books 1850–58.
- Diocese of Derry and Raphoe grant books 1812–51.
- Diocese of Ossory grant books 1848–51.

Indexes to all the wills destroyed in 1922 are available. A full set is available at the National Archives of Ireland (NAI). Many indexes were published prior to destruction, and may be found in research libraries. These publications are also available online (see below). Although the actual wills are lost, the published indexes may still be useful. They are likely to record the testator's name, abode, the year of probate, and perhaps his status or occupation. The most important published indexes include:

- Vicars, Arthur, ed. *Index to Prerogative wills 1536–1810*, Dublin: E. Ponsonby, 1897. Reprinted Baltimore: Genealogical Publishing, 1987. Available online at **www.origins.net**, **www.ancestry.co.uk**, and **www.ajmorris.com/dig/toc/index.htm**

- *Index to the act or grant books and to the original wills of the diocese of Dublin (c. 1638) to the year 1800*, Baltimore: Genealogical Publishing, 1997. Reprinted from Deputy Keeper of Ireland's *Reports* 1894–9. Now available on CD as *Index of wills and marriage licences for Dublin Diocese to 1800*, Flyleaf Press, nd. Available online at **www.origins. net**.

- Phillimore, W. P. W., & Thrift, Gertrude. *Indexes to Irish Wills*. 5 vols in 1. Baltimore: Genealogical Publishing, 1970. Originally published 1909–1920. v. 1. Ossory, Leighlin, Ferns, Kildare. v. 2. Cork and Ross, Cloyne. v. 3. Cashel and Emly, Waterford and Lismore, Killaloe and Kilfenora, Limerick, Ardfert and Aghadoe. v. 4. Dromore, Newry and Mourne. v. 5. Derry and Raphoe. Available online at **www.ancestry.co.uk** and **www. origins.net**

Abstracts of most of the destroyed Prerogative Court wills pre-1800 were made in the nineteenth century by Sir William Betham. His notebooks are now in NAI. Vicars's *Index to Prerogative Wills* can be used as an index to them.

After the destruction of the Irish Public Record Office, an attempt was made to identify all surviving wills. Many wills can be found amongst the records of charities and other organizations. Others are held amongst the

From The Times, *1 July 1922. The Four Courts housed the Irish Public Record Office and the Probate Registry.*

THE WRECKED FOUR COURTS.

BUILDING LAID DESOLATE.

FIREMEN POWERLESS.

One of our Special Correspondents who was in Dublin all day yesterday, and crossed by the night boat to Holyhead, telephoned early this morning the following graphic description of the scene in the wrecked Four Courts building, which he visited after the surrender.

(From Our Special Correspondent.)

HOLYHEAD, July 1.

About an hour after the surrender of the Four Courts I went inside.

The circular hall under the dome, and the passages and rooms adjoining, were all filled with *débris*, which was blazing fiercely. At the north end the rim of the supporting edge of the dome was alight, and burning very fast. The columns supporting the dome to the rear, or some of them, were out of contact with the rim of the dome at the top, and the consequence is that the whole fabric is liable to collapse at any moment.

The east wing of the building collapsed at an early stage after the explosion, and dense clouds of black smoke shot up into the air. The whole of the forecourt was filled with barbed wire. There was a tremendous amount of damage outside in the lower front of the building by bursting shells. One of the first columns supporting the portico has had a direct hit from a shell, and has had practically three-quarters of its length knocked off.

A fire-engine and an escape arrived in front of the building about 3 o'clock, but it was quite impossible to make any attempt to attack the fire, the situation being hopeless. One feature of the fire was the complete destruction of the records. This was made plain by the showers of burnt paper which came down in the street. A witness of the scene, who had visited the ruins of Reims Cathedral, said that the havoc was worse in Dublin.

The explosion is supposed to have been due to fire caused by a shell falling on a large stock of gelignite. The Free State soldiers were taken completely by surprise, but it is not definitely known whether a mine was fired by the rebels or whether explosives they had accumulated were caught by the flames.

The Irish Wills Index Database.

archives of solicitors and private estates. The Inland Revenue compiled will registers covering the period 1828–39; there are also Inland Revenue indexes to administrations 1828–79. A comprehensive index to wills and related records (including the will and grant books mentioned above) is available at NAI, and online at:

- Irish Wills Index 1484–1858 **www.origins.net/help/aboutio-wills.aspx**

For more information on probate records held by the National Archives of Ireland, visit:

- National Archives of Ireland: Wills & Testamentary Records **www.nationalarchives.ie/genealogy/testamentary.html**

Apart from the indexes mentioned above, few official pre-1858 probate records survive for Northern Ireland. The Public Record Office of Northern Ireland (PRONI) does, however, hold an index of wills found in its collections of estate and solicitors archives. For details of this index, and of other relevant material held, see its guide to:

- Wills and Testamentary Records **www.proni.gov.uk/07_-_your_family_tree_series_-_wills_and_testamentary_records.pdf**

Click 'Local History Series: 1'

Since 1858, Irish wills have been proved in the Principal and District Registries of the Probate Court (before 1877) or High Court (after 1877). From 1918, there are separate indexes for Northern Ireland. The original wills were held by the Irish Public Record Office when it was destroyed, and all pre-1900 wills were consequently lost. However, the district registries had made fairly full transcripts of wills before sending the originals to the Principal Registry. These 'will books' survive; they are now held by NAI and (for Northern Ireland) PRONI. Original wills are currently transferred from the district registries to NAI when they are twenty-five years old, or, in the case of Northern Ireland, to PRONI when they are seven years old.

Calendars of wills and administrations for the whole of Ireland were compiled annually between 1858 and 1921, and are held by NAI and PRONI. There is a consolidated index for 1858–77. The calendars for Armagh, Belfast and Londonderry registries, 1858–1919 and 1922–43, together with digitized copies of original wills 1858–1900, can be searched online at

- Will Calendars
  www.proni.gov.uk/index/search_the_archives/will_calendars.htm

For a detailed online guide to Irish wills, see

- Irish Ancestors: Wills
  www.irishtimes.com/ancestor/browse/records/wills

A full listing of surviving collections of wills, including details of indexes, is included in:

- Grenham, John. *Tracing your Irish Ancestors*. 3rd ed. Gill & Macmillan, 2006.

Isle of Man

Manx wills were proved in the Archdeaconry Court of the Isle of Man, or in its superior court, the Consistory Court of the Bishop of Sodor and Man. The island was within the Province of York, so some wills may also be found in PCY. Both courts had jurisdiction throughout the island, alternating for part of the year. After 1874, the Consistory Court had sole jurisdiction. Since 1885, wills have been proved in the High Court of Justice. Probate records prior to 1911 are held by the Manx Museum. Some have been transcribed and indexed on the Manx Notebook webpage:

- Index to Wills
  www.isle-of-man.com/manxnotebook/famhist/wills/index.htm

More recent probate records are held by the Isle of Man's Deeds and Probate Registry **www.gov.im/registries/general/deedsandpro.xml**. It is also worth noting that the Latter Day Saints Family History Library have microfilms of many Manx wills.

Probate law on Man had many differences from the law in England. For a brief discussion, see the Manx Notebook's page on:

- Wills and Laws of Inheritance
  www.isle-of-man.com/manxnotebook/famhist/genealogy/wills.htm

Scotland

The Scottish system of inheritance has important differences from that which operates in England. Between the sixteenth century and 1823, testaments were 'confirmed' (not 'proved') by Commissary courts. These courts were civil rather than ecclesiastical institutions, although their jurisdictional boundaries were based on medieval dioceses.

Until 1868, the Scottish law of inheritance imposed much tighter restrictions on the powers of testators than those which existed in England. The law of primogeniture was applied rigidly to the descent of all heritable property, that is, real estate, which could not be left by will. It descended to the eldest son, or, if there was no son, was divided equally between daughters. If there were no children, the widow inherited.

The descent of moveable property was also strictly controlled. A third went automatically to the widow, and a third to children (other than the eldest son). Only the final third could be bequeathed. Partly for that reason, and partly due to the poverty of the country, there are relatively few testamentary documents, especially prior to the nineteenth century. The law was amended in 1868, and bequests of real property became possible.

Testaments had to be confirmed by an appropriate court. There were twenty-two Commissary courts throughout Scotland; details are given on the Scotland's People site (see below). Their boundaries are mapped by Cecil Humphery-Smith in his *Phillimore atlas and index of parish registers* (3rd ed., Phillimore, 2003). Further details are given in Jeremy Gibson and Else Churchill's *Probate jurisdictions: where to look for wills* (5th ed., Federation of Family History Societies, 2002). The Principal Commissariot Court of Edinburgh had jurisdiction over the whole of Scotland, as well as over its own district, and over Scots resident abroad. If a testator owned goods in more than one commissariot, his testament had to be confirmed in Edinburgh. Executors did not necessarily use their local commissariot. Testaments could be confirmed in any of these courts, without geographical restriction.

In 1824, testamentary jurisdiction was transferred to Sheriff courts, although it took some years for the transfer to be fully effective. Their jurisdictional boundaries roughly followed the county boundaries of the day.

Confirmation required the court to draw up a document known as a testament. Strictly speaking, the document bequeathing moveable property was actually a testament; wills only bequeathed real property, and hence can only be found after 1868. However, the word 'will' is commonly used to refer to both types of document, and that usage will be adopted here.

There are two types of testament. The testament testamentar was prepared when a testator had left a will. It included four elements: the introductory clause, an inventory of the deceased's goods, the confirmation clause, and a copy of the will itself. If the will has not been copied, there will be an indication of where a copy can be found – usually in the court's own registry of deeds.

The second type of testament is the testament dative, drawn up by the court when there was no will. It comprises three parts: the introductory clause, an inventory of the deceased's goods, and the confirmation of the executor, who would usually be a relative, but who might be a creditor. There are more testaments dative than there are testaments testamentar.

All Scottish testamentary documents which have been confirmed by a court have been digitized, and are available on a pay-per-view site:

- Scotland's People **www.scotlandspeople.gov.uk**

There are 611,000 index entries on this site; the documents date from 1513 to 1901. Index entries list surnames, forenames, titles, occupations and abodes (where given) of the deceased. They also note the court which granted confirmation, and the date. This database renders it unnecessary to know which court a will was proved in in order to obtain a copy.

Older wills may be in an unfamiliar handwriting. If you need help in reading them, use the tutorials (including one on eighteenth-century testaments) provided by:

- Scottish Handwriting **www.scottishhandwriting.com**

Another problem may be posed by the language used in old wills. Many of the words used are now obsolete. Help with this problem is offered by:

- Scottish Archive Network: the Glossary
  www.scan.org.uk/researchrtools/glossary.htm

The original documents are held in the National Archives of Scotland (NAS); however, since they are available in digital format, they are not normally produced for inspection. Consequently, the various indexes to them formerly published by the Scottish Record Society are redundant if you are using Scotland's People database.

Post-1901 confirmation records are also held by the NAS, unless still retained by the relevant sheriff's clerk. There are annual consolidated calendars of confirmations, printed up to 1959, but on microfiche from 1960.

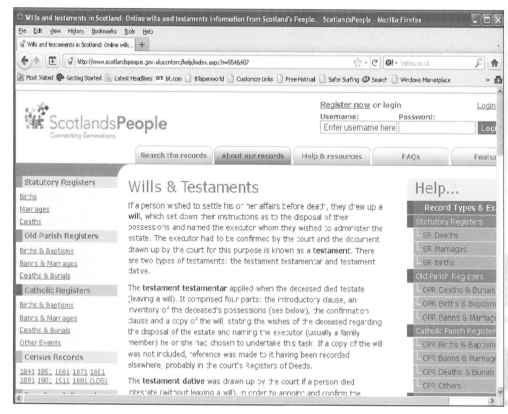

Scotland's People website: a vital resource for all Scottish researchers.

A computerized index, 1985–1996, is available in the Historical Search Room (although not online). Calendars are also available at the Mitchell Library, Glasgow, up until 1936.

An alternative means of obtaining information from Scottish wills is provided by the microfilmed copies held by the Latter Day Saints' Family History Library, which are available through its world-wide branch network. These are not complete; for details, see:

- Family Search; Scotland Probate Records
  https://wiki.familysearch.org/en/Scotland_Probate_Records

After 1858, succession to Scottish property of persons resident in England could be secured by resealing. The English probate court would send a copy of its grant to the Commissariot Court in Edinburgh. Conversely, succession to English property of persons resident in Scotland could be secured by the reverse procedure. These resealed probates are included in the Scotland's

People database up to 1901, and listed in the calendars of confirmations thereafter. They are also listed in the appendices to the English National Probate Calendar between 1858 and 1876.

Many wills of Scottish soldiers and airmen were passed by the War Office to the Commissary Office in Edinburgh. These were written either in their passbooks, or on official army forms. They dated from 1857 to 1966, although most are from the two world wars. Not all of these were confirmed, and therefore do not appear in the Scotland's People database. An online index to them is available. They have been digitized, but images are not available online. For details, see:

- National Archives of Scotland: Searching for soldiers' and airmen's wills **www.nas.gov.uk/guides/searchSoldiersWills.asp**

The descent of land by primogeniture was recorded in retours, or services of heirs. These are the returns made by juries called to determine the right of vassals to inherit landed property. An NAS guide provides full details:

- Inheriting Land and Buildings
  www.nas.gov.uk/guides/inheriting.asp

The strict application of the law of primogeniture before 1867 meant that testators sometimes sought a way to avoid its requirements. One way of doing this was to establish a trust. Ownership was transferred in the owners' lifetime to a group of trustees, who were instructed to use it for specified purposes. Trust dispositions and settlements (sometimes referred to as TD&S) could give the grantor complete control over the land during his lifetime, but transferred it to whoever he wanted to inherit on his death. These deeds could also include disposition of moveable property, and were normally registered after death – although such registration was not compulsory. Registration could take place in a number of different places. Great landowners were likely to use the deeds register of the Court of Session. Others could use registers of deeds maintained by sheriffs' courts, commissary courts (up to 1809), and royal burghs. For details, consult the NAS guide to deeds **www.nas.gov.uk/guides/deeds.asp**.

The administration of trusts was recorded in trust sederunt books. Where these survive, they may provide much useful information. They are described on the Scottish Archive Network's Knowledge Base:

- Trust Sederunt Books **www.scan.org.uk/knowledgebase/topics/ trustsederuntbooks_topic.htm**

Chapter 9

WHERE CAN I FIND OTHER SOURCES OF PROBATE INFORMATION?

Estate Records

Most pre-1858 wills are likely to be found in the archives of ecclesiastical probate courts. However, there are a number of other places that are worth searching. Wills were important documents for gentlemen with estates to administer. They are likely to have retained copies of wills and other probate documents related to their family and estate. Revoked wills may also have been retained. These documents are frequently encountered amongst estate records. For example, there are over two hundred references to wills in the online catalogue of the Museum of English Rural Life **www. reading.ac.uk/merl**. There are many wills amongst the archives of the Hole family in Devon Record Office.

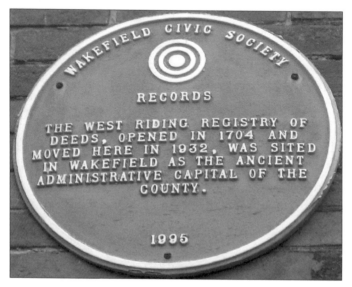

The West Riding Registry of Deeds.
(Courtesy of Mike Kerby)

Wills were important documents in estate archives, because they frequently provided evidence of title to landed property. They were therefore treated as title deeds. The registration of deeds of title made it much easier to prove title to landed property. Consequently, in the late seventeenth and early eighteenth centuries, deeds registries were established in a number of regions: Yorkshire, Middlesex, and the Bedford Levels. Many wills were registered in these registries. For a detailed discussion, see:

- Sheppard, F., & Belcher, V. 'The deeds registries of Yorkshire and Middlesex', *Journal of the Society of Archivists* 6 (5), 1980, pp. 274–86
- Middlesex Deeds Registry 1709–1838 **www.cityoflondon.gov.uk** (Search '1709')
- West Riding Registry of Deeds **www.archives.wyjs.org.uk/wyjs-archives-w-r-registry-u.asp**
- East Riding Registry of Deeds **www.eyfhs.org.uk/content/resources/ treasurehouse/register_of_deeds.pdf**

Death Duty Registers

Another important source of probate information are the death duty registers held by TNA. These were compiled in order to assess liability to three different taxes: legacy, succession, and estate duty. Legacy duty commenced in 1780, but the earliest surviving registers are from 1796. Before 1805, they cover about a quarter of all estates. However, taxes increased, as is usual, and many more estates became liable for duty. By 1857, there should be an entry for all estates valued at over £20. The registers were closed in 1903, when individual files began to be used. Most of the latter have been destroyed. Some registers from the 1890s have also been lost in a fire.

Death duty registers are based on the evidence provided by wills, details of which were submitted by all probate courts. They can therefore help you to identify the court in which your ancestor's will was proved – which is particularly useful for pre-1857 wills. The information provided in the registers includes:

- the name of the deceased
- his address and last occupation
- the date of the will, and the place and date of probate
- the names, addresses and occupations of executors
- details of estates, legacies, trustees, legatees, annuities, and duty paid

They may also include dates of death, and information concerning beneficiaries and next of kin. It was important to record information relating to the relationships of beneficiaries and testators, since legacies to certain close kin were exempt from taxation. From 1815, however, only bequests to spouses were exempt. Duty was not necessarily payable immediately, and consequently the registers were annotated for many years after entries were first made, and may include, for example, details of the deaths of spouses and beneficiaries, births of posthumous children and grandchildren, changes of address, references to any legal disputes, and cross-references to other entries in the registers. Such information may be vital for the family historian.

The registers include valuations of decedents' estates. These valuations should be treated with caution. They were based on bequests made in wills, rather than on inventories of goods. Until 1853, they did not include realty. Between 1853 and 1893, legacy duty applied to personalty, and succession duty applied to realty. In order to get a full picture in this period, it is necessary to examine the registers for both taxes, and to add together the two separate valuations in order to discover the total valuation of an estate.

The registers are held by TNA, class IR26. Indexes can be found in IR27, although they do not cover the Succession Duty registers. These indexes are now available online from Find My Past, and can indirectly be used as an index to all wills and administrations which attracted death duties during this period. Consult Find My Past's Knowledge Base at **www.findmypast. co.uk/helpadvice/knowledge-base/wills-divorces** for details.

The registers themselves are also available online, but only for the period 1796–1811. During this period, separate registers were kept for records from PCC and from the 'country courts'. The clerks of probate courts entered extracts of wills and administrations on separate sheets for each individual. These sheets were sent to the Board of Stamps, where they were bound into registers. The Board's clerks made many subsequent annotations in these registers. The country registers have been digitized at:

- Documents Online: Death Duty Registers (1796–1811)
  www.nationalarchives.gov.uk/documentsonline/death-duty.asp

From 1812, the procedure changed. The staff of the Legacy Duty Office were themselves responsible for entering details in the registers, from copies of wills and accounts of administrations sent in by the ecclesiastical courts. The registers became more concise. Until 1857, four separate registers were compiled annually. Wills and administrations had their own separate registers, and the division between PCC and the country courts was maintained. Between 1858 and 1881, following the abolition of ecclesiastical probate courts, only two registers were kept: for wills and administrations. These were merged in 1882. Full details of these and later documents can be found by searching IR26 and IR27 in TNA's catalogue **www.national archives.gov.uk/catalogue**. See also TNA's guide to:

- Looking for records of a death duty between 1796 and 1903 **www. nationalarchives.gov.uk/records/looking-for-person/deathduty.htm**

Indexes to Death Duty Registers can be searched at Find My Past.

The registers provide a valuable substitute for the wills destroyed in the World War Two bombing of Exeter. Even more usefully, the copies of wills sent to the Estate Duty Office by probate courts for the counties of Cornwall, Devon, and Somerset, are now in the record offices for those counties (copies for other counties have been destroyed). For Somerset, see:

- Hawkings, David T., ed. *Index of Somerset Estate Duty Office wills and letters of administration 1805–1811*. Weston-super-Mare: Galloway, 1995.
- Hawkings, David T., ed. *Index of Somerset Estate Duty Office Wills 1812–1857*. 2 pts, Weston-super-Mare: Galloway, 1995. Online at **www1.somerset.gov.uk/archives/ASP/ddedsearch.htm**

Microfilm of the registers and indexes in IR26 and IR27 are available through the world-wide branches of the Latter Day Saints' Family History Library. For details, visit

- Family Search: Estate Duty Registers **https://wiki.familysearch.org/en/Estate_Duty_Registers**

In addition to the registers, TNA also holds papers related to the administration of death duties, and especially relating to contentious cases.

Bank of England Will Extracts

The Inland Revenue was not the only institution that needed to see extracts from wills. The Bank of England managed stock in public funds, and needed proof of entitlement in order to transfer monies invested from testators to legatees. Executors had to submit extracts from the wills of testators in order for heirs to receive their inheritance.

Investment in the public funds was often seen as a secure means of saving for old age, or as a suitable way to use surplus income. Fundholders were drawn from every social class – servant girls to peers. The monetary value of stockholdings was frequently quite low. Londoners, immigrants (especially Dutch), and religious minorities were particularly numerous amongst the stockholders, although they came from every part of the British Isles and its colonies. The Bank's will extracts (which also include abstracts of orders relating to bankrupts and lunatics) are held by the Society of Genealogists. There are 60,523 entries in the index, which is available online at:

- Bank of England Wills Extracts Index 1717–1845
  www.findmypast.co.uk/content/sog/wills-extracts.html

Navy Office Wills

The Navy Office was another collector of wills. Seamen frequently died when they were still entitled to pay, or to prize money. It was easy for fraudsters to impersonate the executors of deceased seamen, and to claim their back pay and effects. Consequently, in 1786 the office of Inspector of Wills was established. The Inspector was tasked with ensuring that executors received what was due to them. Proof of entitlement was provided by seamen's wills, which were usually written on printed forms, and deposited in the Navy Office by the seamen themselves. When the Office received a will, a cheque, that is, a certificate, was sent to the executor. When the testator died, the executor claimed any moneys due by returning the cheque to the Navy Office. The cheque was then passed to a probate court, the executor paid, and the will noted with the name of the relevant court. Some 19,927 wills were collected. They are now in TNA (ADM48/1-105, with indexes in ADM142/1-14). The indexes are available online at **www.national archives.gov.uk/documentsonline/digital-microfilm.asp**. The wills themselves can be downloaded from TNA's Documents Online pay-per-view site:

- Wills of Royal Naval Seamen (1786–1882)
  www.nationalarchives.gov.uk/documentsonline/seamenswills.asp

The indexes in ADM142 give not only the name of the seaman, and the date of his death, they also include the name, address and relationship of the executor or administrator of the will, and cover the period up to 1909. ADM142 is also available online (at no cost); however, it cannot be searched automatically. It is necessary to download images of entire volumes, and scroll through them until you find the appropriate entry. Visit:

- Digital Microfilm **www.nationalarchives.gov.uk/documentsonline/ digital-microfilm.asp**

TNA also holds a variety of related records. Applications by next of kin for the unpaid wages or pensions of Royal Navy and Royal Marine Officers, and of civilian naval employees, are in ADM45 for 1830–60. Sometimes these include supporting documents, including wills. Applications can be searched by name in TNA's online catalogue. Similar documents for ratings, 1800–1860, are in ADM44 (with indexes in ADM141). There are also registers of deceased ratings for 1859–78, indicating whether a will exists, in ADM154, and registers of probates, letters of administration, and so on relating to deceased pensioners, 1830–1915, in PMG50. Earlier extracts from the wills of Royal Marines can be found in ADM96/524. These cover the period 1740–64.

Soldiers' Wills

For soldiers, it may be worth consulting the casualty returns in WO25/1359-2407. These cover the period 1809–55, and sometimes include both wills and inventories. Applications for pensions from widows also frequently included wills, administrations, and other useful documents, such as birth, marriage and death certificates. Widows' correspondence is in WO43, but the documents they sent with their applications are in WO42; these documents cover the period 1755–1908.

For a much earlier period, it may be worth consulting the collection of wills in E315/483. These are copies of wills made from PCC will registers, and used by the interregnum government between 1648 and 1659 to settle areas of pay.

Roman Catholic Wills

A rather different purpose was served by the enrolment of Roman Catholic wills on the Close rolls (TNA C54) after 1716. This was an era of penal legislation against adherents to the Pope. Their wills, together with enrolments in the Treasury of Receipt, the Close Rolls, and the Recovery Rolls, are listed in:

- 'Some wills in the Public Record Office', *Genealogist* New series 1, 1884, pp. 266–7; 2, 1885, pp. 59–60 & 279–82; 3, 1886, pp. 122–3, 185–7, & 220–2.

The British in India

Of much greater significance are the wills in the British Library's Oriental and India Office collections. Between the seventeenth and the twentieth centuries, many British people took service with the East India Company, or, in the later period, with the colonial government. Many died in India. Their wills were proved in local courts, initially run by the Company. Many registers survive; for details, consult:

- British Library: Help for researchers: Wills and Administrations **www.bl.uk/reshelp/findhelpregion/asia/india/indiaofficerecords familyhistory/willsandadministrations/willsadmin.html**

A detailed listing of probate records is provided in Chapter 9 of:

- Jolly, Emma. *Tracing Your British India Ancestors.* Pen & Sword, 2012.

Other Small Collections

A variety of other minor will collections can be found in TNA. Collections of overseas wills include the following:

- FO626 Wills proved in the Smyrna Consulate Court, 1820–1929
- FO917 Wills proved in the Shanghai Supreme Consular Court 1857–1941
- FO678/2729-931 Wills proved in the Chinese Consulate Courts 1837–1951
- FO184/14 Wills proved in the Russian Consulate 1817–66
- FO335/164 Wills proved in the Tunis Consulate 1866–85

These and some other collections are indexed in:

- *A list of wills, administrations, etc., in the Public Record Office, London,* Baltimore: Magna Carta Book Co., 1968.

Many wills in these collections can also be identified through TNA's online catalogue. It is also worth reading:

- The National Archives: Wills and Probate Records **www.national archives.gov.uk/records/research-guides/wills-and-probate-records.htm**

106

The British Library is another potential source of wills. Many strays can be found by consulting:

- British Library Manuscripts Catalogue
  www.bl.uk/catalogues/manuscripts/INDEX.asp

This includes, for example, a herald's collection of the eighteenth-century wills of the incumbents of St Albans Archdeaconry, indexes of wills of the Island of Barbados, and collections of the wills of particular families, such as the Hales of Kings Walden (Hertfordshire) and the Bakers of Leicester.

It is also worth noting that the voluminous *Reports of the Commissioners for Inquiry concerning charities* (32 vols, HMSO, 1819–1840) contain numerous extracts from wills. Charities themselves are likely to have retained copies of the wills of their major benefactors. The wills by which local charities were founded can frequently be found amongst parish and municipal records.

FURTHER READING

Introductory reading

A number of works provide useful introductions to probate records. For local historians, the best is:

Arkell, Tom, Evans, Nesta, & Goose, Nigel, eds. *When death do us part: understanding and interpreting the probate records of early modern England.* Leopards Head Press, 2004.

Wills in PCC are the major focus of:

Grannum, Karen, & Taylor, Nigel, eds. *Wills & probate records: a guide for family historians.* 2nd ed. National Archives, 2009.

See also:

Riden, Philip, ed. *Probate records and the local community*, Alan Sutton, 1985.

Cox, Nancy & Jeff. 'Probate inventories: the legal background', *Local historian*, 16, 1984, pp. 133–45 & 217–27.

Cox, Nancy & Jeff. 'Valuations in probate inventories', *Local historian*, 16, 1984, pp. 467–77; 17, 1986, pp. 85–100.

For a valuable introduction to probate accounts, and a full index to them nationwide, see:

Spufford, Peter, et al, eds. *Index to the probate accounts of England and Wales.* 2 vols. British Record Society 112–3. 1999.

For a useful discussion of the role of probate courts in the sixteenth century, see the chapter on 'testamentary administration and litigation' in:

Houlbrooke, Ralph. *Church courts and the people during the English Reformation, 1520–1570.* Oxford University Press, 1979.

For an introduction to the international dimension, consult:

Van Der Woude, & Schuurman, Anton, eds. *Probate inventories: a new source for the historical study of wealth, material culture, and agricultural development. Papers presented at the Leeuwenborch Conference (Wageningen, 5–7 May, 1980).* 1980.

A detailed listing of probate courts and their records, including maps of the various jurisdictions, is provided by Gibson and Churchill. This volume also lists numerous indexes, both published and unpublished, which are therefore not listed in the present volume. See:

Gibson, J.S.W., & Churchill, Else. *Probate jurisdictions: where to look for wills.* 5th ed. Federation of Family History Societies, 2002.

This volume is updated by:

Andrew Millard's Genealogy: Recent Indexes to English, Welsh, Scottish and Irish Probate Records **www.dur.ac.uk/a.r.millard/genealogy/probate. php**

The areas covered by probate courts are mapped in:

Humphery-Smith, C.R., ed. *Phillimore atlas and index of parish registers.* 3rd ed. Phillimore, 2003.

For the history of probate during the Civil War and Interregnum, see:

Kitching, Christopher. 'Probate during the Civil War and Interregnum', *Journal of the Society of Archivists,* 5, 1976, pp. 283–93 & 346–56.

Many editions of probate records have glossaries of archaic terms used in them. For a comprehensive overview based on these glossaries, consult:

Raymond, Stuart A. *Words from wills and other probate records: a glossary.* Federation of Family History Societies, 2004.

See also:

Milward, Rosemary. *A glossary of household, farming and trade terms from probate inventories.* 2nd ed. Occasional paper, 1. Derbyshire Record Society, 1983.
Needham, Sue. *A glossary for East Yorkshire and North Lincolnshire probate inventories.* Studies in regional and local history, 3. Hull: University of Hull Dept. of Adult Education, 1984.

Many works based on probate records are in print. Arkell et al (see above) have a useful bibliography. For a list of older works, consult:

Overton, Mark. *A bibliography of British probate inventories.* Dept. of Geography, University of Newcastle upon Tyne, 1983.

Three recent works using probate inventories should be consulted by all local historians:

Overton, Mark, et al. *Production and consumption in English households, 1600–1750.* Routledge, 2004. Based on inventories from Cornwall and Kent.

Muldrew, Craig. *The Economy of obligation: the culture of credit and social relations in early modern England.* Macmillan, 1998.

Weatherill, Lorna. *Consumer behaviour and material culture in Britain 1660–1760.* 2nd ed. Routledge, 1996.

Published Collections of Probate Records

Many probate records have been edited and published. Numerous individual wills and inventories can be found in the journals of local and family history societies. County record societies and others have published many substantial collections of wills and inventories. Full lists of these publications can be found in the present author's series of county bibliographies mentioned above. Only the more substantial collections are listed below. Many of the more recent editions have valuable introductions, which should be consulted by anyone undertaking serious research in probate records. For indexes to published probate records, see:

Jervis, Simon Swynfen. *British and Irish inventories: a list and bibliography of published transcriptions of secular inventories.* Furniture History Society, 2010.

Index to testators of published English late medieval and early Tudor wills and testaments, 1399–1540. CD. Richard III Society, 2008.

Anyone interested in compiling an edition of probate records should first read:

Raymond, Stuart A. 'On the editing of sixteenth and seventeenth century probate records', *Archives* 17(76), 1986, pp. 33–40.

General

Whitelock, Dorothy, ed. *Anglo-Saxon wills.* Cambridge University Press, 1930.

Nichols, John. *A collection of all the wills now known to be extant of the Kings and Queens of England, Princes and Princesses of Wales, and every branch of the royal blood, from the reign of William the Conqueror to that of Henry VII exclusive ...* J. Nichols, 1780.

Furnivall, Frederick J., ed. *The fifty earliest English wills in the Court of Probate, 1387–1439, with a priest's of 1454.* Original series 78. Early English Text Society, 1882. Reprinted Oxford University Press, 1964. Digitized at the Corpus of Middle English Prose and Verse **http://quod.lib.umich.edu/cgi/t/text/text-idx?c=cme;idno=EEWills**

Jacob, E.F., ed. *The register of Henry Chichele, Archbishop of Canterbury, 1414–1443, vol II. Wills proved before the Archbishop or his Commissaries.* Clarendon Press, 1938.

Boatwright, Lesley, & Hammond, Peter William, eds. *The Logge register of Prerogative Court of Canterbury Wills, 1479–1486.* 2 vols. Knaphill: Richard III Society, 2008.

Nichols, John Gough, & Bruce, John, ed. *Wills from Doctors Commons: a selection from the wills of eminent persons proved in the Prerogative Court of Canterbury, 1495–1695.* Camden Society Old Series 83. 1863.

Lea, J. Henry, ed. *Abstracts of wills in the Prerogative Court of Canterbury at Somerset House, London, England. Register Soame, 1620.* New England Historic Genealogical Society, 1904.

Brigg, William, ed. *Genealogical abstracts of wills proved in the Prerogative Court of Canterbury: Register Wootton, 1658.* 7 vols. Leeds: the author, 1894–1914.

North, Dorothy, & Wagner, Henry, eds. *Huguenot wills and administrations in England and Ireland 1617–1849.* 2 vols. Huguenot Society of Great Britain and Ireland, Publications 60. 2007.

Brock, Susan, & Honigman, E.A.J., eds. *Playhouse wills, 1558–1642: an anthology of wills by Shakespeare and his contemporaries.* Manchester University Press, 1993.

Particular Families

Alderman

Alderman, Bob, Alderman, Neil, & Alderman, Mari. *Early Alderman Wills in Northamptonshire (152 –1858).* Corsham: the authors, 2008.

Hatley

Hatley, R.V., ed. *The Hatley wills, 1528–1800.* Antelope, 2003.

Ledward

Ledward, Kenneth S., ed. *Pre-1858 wills, inventories and administrations relating to the surname 'Ledward' and preserved at the Cheshire Record Office.* Ormskirk: Salt Oak 1998

Unton

Nichols, John Gough, ed. *The Unton inventories, relating to Wadley and Faringdon, Co. Berks., in the years 1596 and 1620.* Berkshire Ashmolean Society, 1841.

Wayman

Bloom, J. Harvey, ed. *Wayman wills and administrations preserved in the Prerogative Court of Canterbury, 1383–1821.* Wallace Gandy, 1922.

Places

Bedfordshire see also *Lincolnshire*

McGregor, Margaret, ed. *Bedfordshire wills proved in the Prerogative Court of Canterbury, 1383–1548.* Publications of the Bedfordshire Historical Record Society, 58, 1979.

Cirket, A.F., ed. 'English wills, 1498–1526', *Publications of the Bedfordshire Historical Record Society*, 37, 1957, pp. 1–82 & 169–90. From the Archdeaconry of Bedford.

Bell, Patricia, ed. *Bedfordshire wills, 1480–1519.* Publications of the Bedfordshire Historical Record Society, 45. 1966. Latin wills from the Archdeaconry of Bedford.

There are many published editions of probate records.

Bell, Patricia L., ed. *Bedfordshire wills 1484–1533*. Publications of the Bedford-shire Historical Record Society, 76. 1997. From the Archdeaconry of Bedford.

Bell, Patricia L., ed. *Bedfordshire wills 1531–1539*. Bedfordshire Family History Society, 2005.

Ruscoe, George, ed. *Bedfordshire wills 1537–1545, including probate and other cases from the Archdeacon of Bedford's Court*. Bedfordshire Family History Society, 2010.

Freeman, C.E., ed. 'Elizabethan inventories', *Publications of the Bedfordshire Historical Record Society* 32. 1952, pp. 92–107.

Emmison, F.G., ed. 'Jacobean household inventories', *Publications of the Bedfordshire Historical Record Society*, 20, 1938, pp. 1–241.

Cullett-White, James. *Inventories of Bedfordshire country houses 1714–1830*. Publications of the Bedfordshire Historical Record Society, 74. 1995. Inventories of 18 major landowners.

Turner, F. A. Page, ed. 'The Bedfordshire wills and administrations proved at Lambeth Palace and in the Archdeaconry of Huntingdon', *Bedfordshire Historical Record Society* 2, 1914, p. 3–59. For 1379–1627.

Berkshire

Mortimer, Ian, ed. *Berkshire probate accounts, 1583–1712*. Berkshire Record Society 4. Berkshire Record Office, 1999.

Buckinghamshire see also *Lincolnshire*

Elvey, E.M., ed. *The courts of the Archdeaconry of Buckingham, 1483–1523*. Buckinghamshire Record Society, 19. 1975. Includes 250 wills.

Reed, Michael, ed. *Buckinghamshire probate inventories 1661–1714*. Buckingham-shire Record Society, 24. 1988.

Cambridgeshire

Cambridge

George J. Gray, & William Mortlock Palmer. *Abstracts from the Wills and Testamentary Documents of Printers, Binders, and Stationers of Cambridge, from 1504 to 1699*. Bibliographical Society, 1915.

Cheshire see also *Lancashire*

Price, W.H., ed. 'Calendar of wills, inventories, administration bonds, citations, accounts and depositions in testamentary suits preserved in the Diocesan Registry of Chester, 1701–1800', in *Miscellanies relating to Lancashire and Cheshire* 5. Lancashire and Cheshire Record Society 52. 1906.

Ashton on Mersey

Groves, Jill, ed. *Ashton-on-Mersey and Sale wills: wills and probate inventories from two Cheshire townships.* 3 pts. Sale: Northern Writers Advisory Services, 1999–2002. Pt. 1, 1600–1650. Pt. 2, 1651–1700. Pt. 3: 1701–60.

Bowdon

Groves, Jill, ed. *Bowdon wills: wills and probate inventories from a Cheshire township.* 3 vols. Sale: Northern Writers Advisory Service, 1997. Pt. 1. 1600–1650. Pt. 2. 1651–1689. Pt. 3. 1690–1760.

Christleton

Bland, Tony, ed. *Wills & Inventories with related documents for Christleton, Tarvin, Tattenhall & Waverton for the period 1546–1650.* 5 vols. Tattenhall: Four Parishes Research Group, 2002–6.

Dunham Massey

Groves, Jill, ed. *Dunham Massey Wills: Part 1, 1600–1640.* Northern Writers Advisory Service, 2008.

Hale

Grove, Jill, ed. *Hale Wills: Wills And Probate Inventories from a Cheshire Township.* 2 vols. Northern Writers Advisory Service, 2005.

Malpas

Pearson, Mary, ed. *The wills and inventories of the ancient parishes of Malpas, Tilston and Shocklach and their townships in the county of Chester from 1508 to 1603.* 2 vols. Malpas and District Local History Group, 2005. Further volumes cover 1603–1625.

Nantwich

Cockroft, Jack. *Nantwich Wills: transcripts of wills and inventories.* 6 vols. South Cheshire Family History Society, 1999.

Sale *see* Ashton on Mersey

Shocklach *see* Malpas

Stockport

Phillips, C.B., & Smith, J.H., eds. *Stockport probate records, 1578–1619.* Record Society of Lancashire and Cheshire, 124. 1985.

Phillips, C.B., & Smith, J.H., eds. *Stockport probate records, 1620–1650.* Record Society of Lancashire and Cheshire, 131. 1992.

114

Tarvin *see* **Christleton**

Tattenhall *see* **Christleton**

Tilston *see* **Malpas**

Waverton *see* **Christleton**

Wrenbury
Pixton, Paul B., ed. *Wrenbury wills and inventories, 1542–1661*. Record Society of Lancashire and Cheshire, 144. 2009.

Cornwall
Orme, Nicholas, ed. *Cornish wills, 1342–1540*. Devon & Cornwall Record Society, new series 50. 2007.

Week St Mary
Raymond, S.A. *Seventeenth-century Week St. Mary, Cornwall, including an edition of the probate records 1598 to 1699*. M.A. thesis, University of Adelaide, 1988.

Cumberland see also *Yorkshire*
Ferguson, R.S., ed. *Testamenta Karleolensia: the series of wills from the pre-Reformation registers of the Bishops of Carlisle, 1353–1386*. Cumberland and Westmorland Antiquarian and Archaeological Society Extra series 9. 1893.

Derbyshire
Edwards, David G., ed. *Derbyshire wills proved in the Prerogative Court of Canterbury, 1393–1574*. Derbyshire Record Society, 26. 1998.
Edwards, David G., ed. *Derbyshire wills proved in the Prerogative Court of Canterbury, 1575–1601*. Derbyshire Record Society, 31. 2003.

Chesterfield
Bestall, J.M., & Fowkes, D.V., eds. *Chesterfield wills and inventories, 1521–1603*. Derbyshire Record Society, 1. 1977.
Bestall, J.M., & Fowkes, D.V., eds. *Chesterfield wills and inventories, 1604–1650*. *Derbyshire Record Society*, 28. 2001.

Dore
Hey, David G., *Seke in body but hole in mynd … a selection of wills and inventories of Dore and Totley, 1539–1747*. Dore Village Society, 1990.

Eckington

Wills and inventories for the parish of Eckington in north Derbyshire. Sheffield: Dept. of Adult Education, University of Sheffield, 1995.

New Mills

Bryant, Roger, Lee, Audrey, & Miller, Eileen, eds. *Wills and inventories of New Mills people.* 3 vols. Stockport: New Mills Historical Society, 1995–9. Book 1: 1540–1571 Book 2: 1571–1583. Book 3: 1586–1607.

Devon

Worthy, Charles, ed. *Devonshire wills: a collection of annotated testamentary abstracts ...* 1896.

Dunstan, G.R., ed. *The register of Edmund Lacy, Bishop of Exeter, 1420–1455: register commune, vol.IV.* Devon & Cornwall Record Society, new series 16. 1971. Includes wills proved in the bishop's court.

Cash, Margaret, ed. *Devon inventories of the sixteenth and seventeenth centuries.* Devon & Cornwall Record Society, new series, 11. 1966.

Exeter

Lepine, David, & Orme, Nicholas, eds. *Death and memory in medieval Exeter.* Devon & Cornwall Record Society, new series, 47. 2003. Includes twenty-one Exeter wills, 1244–1349, *etc.*

Crocker, Jannine, ed. *Elizabethan inventories and wills from the Exeter Orphans Court.* Devon & Cornwall Record Society, forthcoming.

Uffculme

Wyatt, Peter, ed. *The Uffculme wills and inventories, 16th to 18th centuries.* Devon & Cornwall Record Society, new series, 40. 1997.

PCC wills from Uffculme can be found in:

Wyatt, Peter, & Stanes, Robert, ed. *Uffculme: a peculiar parish: a Devon town from Tudor times.* Uffculme Archive Group, 1997.

Dorset

Chetnole

Machin, R., ed. *Probate inventories and manorial excepts of Chetnole, Leigh and Yetminster.* Dept. of Extra-Mural Studies, University of Bristol, 1976.

Durham see also Yorkshire

Raine, James, et al, eds. *Wills and inventories illustrative of the history, manners, language, statistics, etc., of the northern counties of England, from the eleventh century downwards.* Surtees Society 2, 38, 112, & 142. 1835–1929. Mainly from the Durham Diocesan registry.

Raine, James, ed. *The injunctions and other ecclesiastical proceedings of Richard Barnes, bishop of Durham, from 1576 to 1587*. Surtees Society 22, 1850. Includes numerous clergy wills.

Darlington
Atkinson, J.A., et al, eds. *Darlington wills and inventories, 1600–1625*. Surtees Society, 201. 1993.

Sunderland
Briggs, Joan, et al, eds. *Sunderland wills and inventories 1601–1650*. Surtees Society, 214. 2010.

Essex
Emmison, F.G., ed. *Essex wills (England). Vol. 1. 1558–1565*. National Geographical Society, 1982.

Emmison, F.G., ed. *Essex wills (England). Vol. 2. 1565–1571. Archdeaconry of Colchester; Archdeaconry of Middlesex; (Essex Division) (preserved in the Essex Record Office, Chelmsford)*. New England Historic Genealogical Society, 1983.

Emmison, F.G., ed. *Essex wills (England). Vol. 3. 1571–1577. Archdeaconry of Colchester; Archdeaconry of Middlesex; (Essex Division) (preserved in the Essex Record Office, Chelmsford)*. New England Historic Genealogical Society, 1986.

Emmison, F.G., ed. *Essex wills: the Archdeaconry Courts, 1577–1584*. E.R.O. publications 96. Essex Record Office, 1987. Further vols. cover 1583–92 (publication 101, 1989); 1591–7 (publication 114, 1991); and 1597–1603 (publication 107, 1990).

Emmison, F.G., ed. *Essex wills: the Bishop of London's Commissary Court 1569–1578*. E.R.O. publications 127. 1994. Further volumes (publication 129, 1995, 137, 1998, & 143, 2000) covers 1578–88, 1587–1599, & 1596–1603.

Emmison, F.G., ed. *Elizabethan life: wills of Essex gentry and yeomen preserved in the Essex Record Office*. Publication 75. Essex Record Office, 1980.

Emmison, F.G., ed. *Elizabethan wills of South West Essex*. Kylin Press, 1983. Proved in the Commissary Court of the Bishop of London.

Walthamstow
Fry, George. S., ed. *Abstracts of wills relating to Walthamstow, co. Essex (1335–1559)*. Walthamstow Antiquarian Society official publication 9. 1921.

Writtle
Steer, F.W., ed. *Farm and cottage inventories of mid-Essex, 1635–1749*. 2nd ed. Phillimore, 1969. For Writtle.

Gloucestershire and Bristol

Bristol

Lang, Sheila, & McGregor, Margaret, eds. *Tudor wills proved in Bristol, 1546–1603*. Bristol Record Society publication, 44. 1993.

McGrath, Patrick, ed. *Bristol wills*. 2 vols. University of Bristol Dept. of Extra-Mural Studies, 1975–8. v.1. 1546–93. v.2. 1597–98.

McGrath, Patrick, ed. *Merchants and merchandise in seventeenth century Bristol*. Bristol Record Society 19. 1955. Includes many wills and inventories.

Wadley, T.P. *Notes or abstracts of the wills contained in the volume entitled the Great Orphan Book and Book of Wills, in the Council House at Bristol*. Bristol & Gloucestershire Archaeological Society, 1886. Covers 1381–1595.

George, Edwin, & George, Stella, eds. *Bristol probate inventories*. 3 vols. Bristol Record Society, 54, 57, & 60. 2002–8. Pt. 1. 1542–1650. Pt. 2. 1657–1689. Pt. 3. 1690–1804.

Burgess, Clive, ed. *The pre-Reformation records of All Saints' Church, Bristol. [Part 3]: Wills, the Halleway Chantry records and deeds*. Bristol Record Society, 56. 2004.

Charlton Kings

Paget, Joan, & Sale, Anthony J.H., eds. *Charlton Kings probate records, 1600–1800*. Charlton Kings Local History Society, 2003.

Cheltenham

Sale, A.J.H., ed. *Cheltenham probate records, 1660–1740*. Gloucestershire record series, 12. Bristol and Gloucestershire Archaeological Society, 1999.

Cirencester

Bishop, G.L., ed. *Wills from Cirencester and district, 1541–1548*. The editor, 1987.

Clifton

Moore, John S., ed. *Clifton and Westbury probate inventories 1609–1761*. Avon Local History Association, 1981.

Frampton Cotterell

Moore, John S., ed. *The goods and chattels of our forefathers: Frampton Cotterell and district probate inventories, 1539–1804*. Phillimore & Co., 1976.

Hampshire

Southampton

Roberts, Edward, & Parker, Karen, eds. *Southampton probate inventories 1447–1575*. 2 vols. Southampton records series, 34–35. 1992.

Yateley

Yateley 1558–1602: transcriptions of wills, admons, and inventories of Yateley. Yateley History Project, 1984.

Hertfordshire see also *Lincolnshire*

Lock, stock and barrel: some Hertfordshire inventories 1610–1650. Hertfordshire sources 12. Hertford: [Hertfordshire County Council], 1978.

Hertford

Adams, Beverley, ed, *Lifestyle and culture in Hertford: wills and inventories for the parishes of All Saints and St Andrew, 1660–1725.* Hertfordshire Record Publications 13. 1997.

Kings Langley

Munby, Lionel M., ed. *Life & death in Kings Langley: wills and inventories, 1498–1659.* Kings Langley: Kings Langley Local History & Museum Society, 1981.

Penwarden, Jill, & Mussett, Maureen, eds. *Where there's a will there's a story: Kings Langley wills and inventories 1660–1800.* Kings Langley Local History and Museum Society, 2004.

St Albans

Flood, S., ed. *St. Albans wills, 1471–1500.* Hertfordshire Record Publications 9. 1993.

Parker, Meryl. *All my worldly goods: an insight into family life from wills and inventories 1447–1742.* 2 pts. Bricket Wood Society, 1991–2004. Pt. 1. *An insight into family life from wills and inventories 1447–1742* introduction by Lionel M. Munby. Pt. 2. *Wills and probate inventories of St Stephen's Parish, St Albans 1418–1700.*

Sarratt

Buller, Philip, & Buller, Barbara. *Pots, platters & ploughs: Sarratt wills & inventories 1435–1832.* Rickmansworth: the authors, [1983?].

Huntingdonshire see *Lincolnshire*

Kent

- Medieval & Tudor Kent P.C.C. & C.C.C. Wills Transcriptions by L.L. Duncan **www.kentarchaeology.org.uk/Research/Libr/Wills/ WillsIntro.htm**

Launay, Jules de, ed. *Weald of East Kent: will abstracts from the Archdeaconry Court of Canterbury, Kent, 1536–1597.* Microfiche. Kent Family History

Society publications 9, 13, 20, 21, 32, 34, 37, 46, 49, 53, 54, 56, 57, 59, 60, & 162. 1981–5. Covers Benenden, Bethersden, Biddenden, Cranbrook, Frittenden, Goudhurst, High Halden, Hawkhurst, Headcorn, Marden, Newenden, Rolvenden, Sandhurst, Smarden, Sataplehurst, Tenterden, Wittersham, and Woodchurch.

Ashford

Hussey, Arthur. *Ashford wills, being abstracts of the wills of residents in the town of Ashford, Kent, 1461–1558, compiled from official records.* Headley Brothers, 1938.

- Abstracts from Ashford, Kent Wills – collected by the late Arthur Ruderman **www.kentarchaeology.org.uk/Research/01/ASH/04/00.htm**

Cranbrook

Launay, Jules de, ed. *Cranbrook wills, 1396–1640, proved in the Diocesan court of Canterbury, and now preserved in Kent Archives Office, Maidstone, Kent, 1396–1640.* Kent Record Collections, 1984.

Sevenoaks

Lansberry, H.C.F., ed. *Sevenoaks wills and inventories in the reign of Charles II.* Kent records 25. Kent Archaeological Society, 1988.

Lancashire

Piccoppe, G.J., ed. *Lancashire and Cheshire wills and inventories from the ecclesiastical court, Chester.* Chetham Society old series 33, 51 & 54. 1857–61. v.1. 1525–54. v.2. 1483–1585. v.3.1596–1639. Supplemented by:

Earwaker, J.P., ed. *Lancashire and Cheshire wills and inventories at Chester, with an appendix of abstracts of wills now lost or destroyed.* Chetham Society New Series 3. 1884.

Earwaker, J.P., ed. *Lancashire and Cheshire wills and inventories, 1572 to 1696, now preserved at Chester, with an appendix of Lancashire and Cheshire wills and inventories proved at York or Richmond, 1542 to 1649.* Chetham Society New Series 28. 1893.

Rylands, J. Paul, ed. *Lancashire and Cheshire wills and inventories 1563 to 1807, now preserved at Chester.* Chetham Society New Series, 37. 1897.

Ferguson, William, ed. *A collection of Lancashire and Cheshire wills not now to be found in any probate registry, 1301–1752.* Lancashire and Cheshire Record Society, 30. 1896.

Bolton

Of good & perfect remembrance: Bolton wills & inventories 1545–1600. 2 vols. Bolton & District Family History Society, 1987–94.

St Helens

Angells to yarwindels: the wills and inventories of twenty-six Elizabethan and Jacobean women living in the area now called St Helens. St Helens Association for Research into Local History, 1999.

Leicestershire see also *Lincolnshire*

Braunstone

Wilshere, Jonathan. *Braunstone probate inventories, 1532 to 1778.* Leicester, 1983.

Evington

Wilshere, Jonathan, ed. *Evington probate inventories, 1557 to 1819.* [2nd ed.] Leicester Research Services Department, 1985.

Glenfield

Wilshere, Jonathan, ed. *Glenfield probate inventories 1542–1831.* Leicester, 1983.

Kirby Muxloe

Wilshere, Jonathan, ed. *Kirby Muxloe probate inventories 1547–1783.* Leicester, 1983.

Ratby

Wilshere, Jonathan, ed. *Ratby probate inventories 1621–1844.* 1984.

Lincolnshire see also *Yorkshire*

Gibbons, Alfred, ed. *Early Lincoln wills: an abstract of all the wills and administrations recorded in the episcopal registers of the old diocese of Lincoln, comprising the counties of Lincoln, Rutland, Northampton, Huntingdon, Bedford, Buckingham, Oxford, Leicester, and Hertford, 1280–1547.* James Williamson, 1888.

Foster, C.W., ed. *Lincoln wills registered in the District Probate Registry at Lincoln.* Lincoln Record Society, 5, 10, & 24. 1914–30. v.1. 1271–1526. v.2. 1505–30. v.3. 1530–32. Covers the whole county, not just Lincoln. Continued by: Hickman, David, ed. *Lincoln wills, 1532–34.* Lincoln Record Society, 89. 2001.

Maddison, A.R. *Lincolnshire wills: first series, A.D.1500–1600.* James Williamson, 1888.

Maddison, A.R. *Lincolnshire wills: second series, A.D.1600–1617.* James Williamson, 1891.

Foster, C.W., ed. *Abstracts of Lincolnshire wills proved in the Prerogative Court of Canterbury.* Supplement to *Lincolnshire notes & queries,* 17–23. 1922–35.

Allington

Pask, Brenda M. *Allington wills & inventories*. [B.M. Pask?], *c.*1989.

Clee

Ambler, R.W., Watkinson, B., & Watkinson, L.A. *Farmers and fishermen: the probate inventories of the ancient parish of Clee, South Humberside, 1536–1742*. Studies in regional and local history, 4. University of Hull School of Adult and Continuing Education, 1987.

Lincoln

Johnstone, J.A., ed. *Probate inventories of Lincoln citizens, 1661–1714*. Lincoln Record Society, 80. 1991.

Market Rasen

Neave, David, ed. *Tudor Market Rasen: life and work in a sixteenth century market town illustrated by probate inventories*. Market Rasen Workers Educational Association / University of Hull Dept. of Adult Education, 1985.

Winteringham

Neave, David, ed. *Winteringham 1650–1760: life and work in a North Lincolnshire village, illustrated by probate inventories*. [Winteringham]: Winteringham W.E.A. Branch, 1984.

London & Middlesex

Darlington, Ida, ed. *London Consistory Court wills, 1492–1547*. London Record Society, 3. 1967.

Sharpe, Reginald R., ed. *Calendar of wills proved and enrolled in the Court of Hustings, London, A.D. 1258 – A.D. 1688, preserved among the archives of the Corporation of the City of London at the Guildhall*. 2 vols. City of London Corporation, 1889.

Eastcheap, St Andrew Hubbard

Burgess, Clive, ed. *The church records of St Andrew Hubbard, Eastcheap, c.1450-c.1570*. London Record Society, 32. 1999. Includes wills and churchwardens accounts.

Hampton

McEleney, H.T., ed. *Hampton Court, Hampton Wick, and Hampton-on-Thames wills and administrations*. Supplement to the *Genealogist*, new series 35–7. 1919–22.

Sunbury
Heselton, Kenneth Y., ed. *Sunbury household effects, 1673–1724 (probate inventories)*. Occasional publication 2. Sunbury and Shepperton Local History Society, 1976.

Norfolk
Wymondham
Wilson, J.H., ed. *Wymondham inventories, 1590–1641*. Creative history from East Anglian sources, 1. Norwich: Centre for East Anglian Studies, 1993.

Northamptonshire see also *Lincolnshire*
Edwards, Dorothy, et al, eds. *Early Northampton wills preserved in the Northamptonshire Record Office*. Northamptonshire Record Society, 42. 2005. From the Archdeaconry of Northampton, 1462–1509.

Northumberland see *Yorkshire*

Nottinghamshire see also *Yorkshire*
Kennedy, P.A., ed. *Nottinghamshire household inventories*. Thoroton Society record series, 22. 1963.

Clayworth
Perkins, Elizabeth R., ed. *Village life from wills & inventories: Clayworth parish, 1670–1710*. Record series, 1. Nottingham: University of Nottingham Centre for Local History, 1979.

Southwell Minster
Leach, Arthur Francis, ed. *Visitations and memorials of Southwell Minster*. Camden Society New Series 48. 1891. Includes 'Wills proved before the Chapter of Southwell, 1470–1541'.

Oxfordshire see also *Lincolnshire*
Weaver, J.R.H., & Beardwood, A., eds. *Some Oxfordshire wills proved in the Prerogative Court of Canterbury, 1393–1510*. Oxfordshire Record Society, 39. 1958.
Havinden, M.A., ed. *Household and farm inventories in Oxfordshire, 1550–1590*. Oxfordshire Record Society, 44. 1965. Also published as Historical Manuscripts Commission joint publication, 10.

Banbury
Brinkworth, E.R.C., & Gibson, J.S.W., eds. *Banbury wills and inventories*. Banbury Historical Society, 13–14. 1976–85. Pt. 1. 1591–1620. Pt. 2. 1621–1650.

Water Eaton

Offord, V.E., ed. *The probate documents of Water Eaton, Oxfordshire, 1592–1730.* Kidlington & District Historical Society, 1986.

Rutland see *Lincolnshire*

Shropshire

Benthall

Trinder, Barrie, & Cox, Nancy, eds. *Miners & mariners of the Severn Gorge: probate inventories for Benthall, Broseley, Little Wenlock, and Madeley, 1660–1764.* Chichester: Phillimore, 2000.

Telford

Trinder, Barrie, & Cox, Jeff, eds. *Yeomen and colliers in Telford: probate inventories for Dawley, Lilleshall, Wellington and Wrockwardine, 1660–1750.* Chichester: Phillimore & Co., 1980.

Somerset

Weaver, F.W., ed. *Somerset medieval wills.* Somerset Record Society, 16, 19, & 21. 1901–5. Series 1. 1383–1500. Series 2: 1501–1530. Series 3. 1531–58.

Shilton, Dorothy O., & Holworthy, Richard, eds. *Medieval wills from Wells deposited in the Diocesan Registry, Wells, 1543 to 1546 and 1554 to 1556.* Somerset Record Society 40. 1925.

Crisp, Frederick Arthur, ed. *Abstracts of Somerset wills copied from the manuscript collections of the late Rev. Frederick Brown.* 6 vols. F.A. Crisp, 1887–90.

Rawlins, S.W., & Jones, I. Fitzroy, eds. *Somerset wills from Exeter.* Somerset Record Society, 62. 1952.

Siraut, Mary, ed. *Somerset wills* extracted by A.J. Monday. Somerset Record Society, 89. 2003.

Webb, A.J., eds. *Somerset wills II* extracted by Miss Olive M. Moger. Somerset Record Society, 94. 2008.

Wellington

Humphreys, A.L. *Materials for the history of the town and parish of Wellington, in the County of Somerset.* H. Gray, 1908–14. Pt. 1. includes wills, 1372–1811, for Wellington and West Buckland.

Staffordshire

Acton Trussell

The inventories and wills of Acton Trussell, 1650–1750. Walton Youth & Community Education Centre, 1995.

Lichfield
Vaisey, D.G., ed. *Probate inventories of Lichfield and district, 1568–1680.* Collections for a history of Staffordshire, 4th series, 5. 1969.

Sedgley
Roper, John S., ed. *Sedgley probate inventories, 1614–1787 (within Sedgley Manor).* Dudley: John S. Roper, [1961]

Smethwick
Bodfish, Mary, ed. *Probate inventories of Smethwick residents, 1647–1747.* Smethwick Local History Society, 1992.

Stafford
'A register of Stafford and other local wills', *Staffordshire Historical Collections* 50. 1926 (1928). pp. 1–56.

Tyrley
Twemlow, F.R. *The manor of Tyrley, in the county of Stafford, down to the outbreak of the Great War in 1914.* Staffordshire Historical Collections 1945–6 (1948). Includes wills and inventories 1553–63.

Suffolk
Tymms, Samuel, ed. *Wills and inventories from the registers of the Commissary of Bury St Edmunds and the Archdeacon of Sudbury.* Camden Society old series 49. 1850.

Sudbury Archdeaconry
Northeast, Peter, & Falvey, Heather, eds. *Wills of the Archdeaconry of Sudbury, 1439– 4: wills from the register 'Baldwyne'.* Suffolk Records Society, 44 & 53. 2001–10. Pt. 1. 1439–1461. Pt. 2. 1461–1474.

Evans, Nesta, ed. *The wills of the Archdeaconry of Sudbury 1630–1635.* Suffolk Records Society, 29. 1987.

Evans, Nesta, ed. *The wills of the Archdeaconry of Sudbury 1636–1638.* Suffolk Records Society, 35. 1993.

Suffolk Archdeaconry
Allen, Marion, ed. *Wills of the Archdeaconry of Suffolk, 1620–1624.* Suffolk Records Society, 31. 1989.

Allen, Marion, ed. *Wills of the Archdeaconry of Suffolk, 1625–1626.* Suffolk Records Society, 37. 1995.

Allen, Marion, & Evans, Nesta R., eds. *Wills from the Archdeaconry of Suffolk, 1629–1636.* New England Historic Genealogical Society, 1986. A further volume covers 1637–40.

Ipswich

Reed, Michael, ed. *The Ipswich probate inventories, 1583–1631*. Suffolk Records Society, 22. 1981.

Newmarket

May, Peter, ed. *Newmarket inventories, 1662–1715*. The author, 1976.

Orford

Wayman, H.W.B., ed. *Suffolk wills (Orford) proved in the Prerogative Court of Canterbury between 1383 and 1800*. English Monumental Inscriptions Society, 1911.

Shotley

Hervey, S.H.A., ed. *Shotley parish records, with illustrations, maps and pedigrees*. Suffolk Green Books 16(2). 1912. Includes 83 wills.

Surrey

Herridge, D.M., ed. *Surrey probate inventories, 1558–1603*. Surrey Record Society 39. 2008.

Surrey wills. Archdeaconry Court, Spage register. Surrey Record Society 5. 1915–20. Also numbered as the Society's *Publications*, 17. Abstracts 1484–90. Reissued on 2 fiche in folder as *Surrey will abstracts* 1. West Surrey Family History Society, [1996]. This is the first of many sets of will abstract fiche issued by West Surrey Family History Society.

Surrey wills. Archdeaconry Court, Herringman register. Surrey Record Society 4. 1915–20. Also numbered as the Society's *Publications*, 3, 7 & 15. Abstracts, 1598–1708.

Sussex

Godfrey, Walter H., ed. *Transcripts of Sussex wills, as far as they relate to ecclesiological and parochial subjects, up to the year 1670*. Sussex Record Society, 41–3. 1935–9.

Hughes, Annabelle, ed. *Sussex clergy inventories 1600–1750*. Sussex Record Society, 91. 2009

Warwickshire

Alcester

Saville, G. Edward. *The seventeenth century inventories of Alcester, Warwickshire*. The author, 1979.

Birmingham

Holt, Richard, Ingram, Janet, & Jarman, John. *Birmingham wills and inventories, 1551–1600*. Birmingham: University of Birmingham Dept. of Extra-mural Studies, 1985.

Foleshill

Upton, Anthony A., ed. *Foleshill probate wills and inventories, 1535–1599.* Foleshill pamphlets, 4. Lighthorne: the author, 1993.

Stoneleigh

Alcock, N.W. *People at home: living in a Warwickshire village, 1500–1800.* Chichester: Phillimore, 1993. Includes inventories for Stoneleigh.

Stratford upon Avon

Jones, Jeanne, ed. *Stratford-upon-Avon inventories, 1538–1699.* Publications of the Dugdale Society, 39–40. 2002–3.

Westmorland see *Yorkshire*

Wiltshire

Marlborough

Williams, Lorelei, & Thomson, Sally, eds. *Marlborough probate inventories 1591–1775.* Wiltshire Record Society, 59. 2007.

Trowbridge

Rogers, Kenneth. *Pre-reformation piety in Trowbridge, Steeple Ashton, and Keevil.* Friends of Trowbridge Museum, 2004. Medieval wills.

Worcestershire

Wanklyn, Malcolm, ed. *Inventories of Worcestershire landed gentry, 1537–1786.* Worcestershire Historical Society, new series, 16. 1998.

Belbroughton

Roper, John S. *Belbroughton, Worcestershire: a selection of wills and probate inventories, 1539–1647.* Dudley: J.S. Roper, 1967.

Chaddesley Corbett

Roper, J.S. *Chaddesley Corbett, Worcestershire, probate inventories with abstracts of wills, 1601–1652.* Dudley: the author, 1971.

Dudley

Roper, John S., ed. *Dudley probate inventories, 1544–1603.* Dudley: [J.S.Roper], 1965–6.

Roper, John S., ed. *Dudley probate inventories (second series) January 1605-April 1685.* Dudley: [J.S.Roper], 1966.

Roper, John S., ed. *Dudley probate inventories (third series), with abstracts of wills and notes from Dudley Parish registers.* Dudley: [John S. Roper], 1968.

Worcester

Dyer, A. D., ed. 'Probate inventories of Worcester tradesmen, 1545–1614', in *Miscellanea II*. Worcestershire Historical Society, new series, 5. 1967, 1–67.

Yorkshire

Raine, James, et al, eds. *Testamenta Eboracensia: or, wills registered at York illustrative of the history, manners language statistics etc of the Province of York, from the year 1300 downwards*. Surtees Society 4, 30, 45, 53, 79 & 106. 1836–1902.

Clay, J.W., ed. *North country wills, being abstracts of wills relating to the counties of York, Nottingham, Northumberland, Cumberland and Westmorland at Somerset House and Lambeth Palace*. Surtees Society, 116 & 121. 1908–12. Vol. 1. 1383 to 1558. Vol. 2. 1558 to 1604.

Stell, Philip, ed. *Probate inventories of the York Diocese, 1350–1500*. York Archaeological Trust, 2006.

Brears, Peter C.D., ed. *Yorkshire probate inventories, 1542–1689*. Yorkshire Archaeological Society record series, 134. 1972.

Clay, John William, ed. *Abstracts of Yorkshire wills in the time of the Commonwealth, at Somerset House, London, chiefly illustrative of Sir William Dugdale's visitation of Yorkshire in 1665–6*. Yorkshire Archaeological and Topographical Association Record Series, 9. 1890.

Abbotside

Thwaite, Hartley, ed. *Abstracts of Abbotside wills 1552–1688*. Yorkshire Archaeological Society record series, 130. 1968.

Barnoldswick

Kirk, G. E., ed. 'Some documents of Barnoldswick manor court of probate', in Whiting, C. E., ed. *Miscellanea vol. VI*. Yorkshire Archaeological Society record series, 118. 1953, 53–84.

Barwick in Elmet

Lumb, George Denison, ed. *Wills, registers and monumental inscriptions of the parish of Barwick in Elmet, Co.York*. Privately printed, 1908.

Crosley

Preston, William E., ed. *Wills proved in the court of the manor of Crosley, Bingley, Cottingley, and Pudsey, in Co. York, with inventories and abstracts of bonds*. Bradford Historical and Antiquarian Society Local Record Series, 1. 1929.

Halifax

Clay, J.W., & Crossley, E.W., eds. *Halifax wills, being abstracts and translations of the wills registered at York from the parish of Halifax*. 2 vols. Privately printed, 1906.

Horbury

Bartlett, K.S., ed. *The wills of Horbury, 1404–1688*. Wakefield Metropolitan District Council, 1979. Two further vols. cover 1688–1757 & 1757–1809.

Knaresborough

Collins, Francis, ed. *Wills and administrations from the Knaresborough court rolls*. Yorkshire Archaeological Society Record Series 104 & 110. 1902–5. For 1506–1668, with separate index of wills, 1640–1858.

Leeds

Lumb, G.D., et al, eds. 'Testamenta Leodiensia', in *Miscellanea* 1, 2 & 3. *Thoresby Society publications* 2, 1891, pp. 98–110; 4, 1895 pp. 1–16 & 139–47; 9, 1899, pp. 246–77. Covers 1391–1531.

Lumb, George Denison, ed. *Testamenta Leodiensia: wills of Leeds, Pontefract, Wakefield, Otley and district, 1553 to 1561*. Thoresby Society 19. 1913.

Lumb, George Denison, ed. *Wills of Leeds, Pontefract, Wakefield, Otley and district, 1539 to 1553*. Thoresby Society 27. 1930.

Richmond Archdeaconry

Raine, James, ed. *Wills and inventories from the Registry of the Archdeaconry of Richmond, extending over portions of the counties of York, Westmerland [sic], Cumberland and Lancaster*. Surtees Society, 26. 1853. For 1442–1579.

Ripon

Fowler, J.T., ed. *Acts of the chapter of the Collegiate Church of Ss Peter and Wilfrid, Ripon, A.D. 1452 to A.D. 1506*. Surtees Society 64. 1875. Includes some wills and inventories not in the Act book.

Rothwell

Cooke, Robert Beilby, ed. 'Wills of the parishes of Rothwell, Saxton, Sherbury in Elmet, Swillington, Thorner, Whitkirk and Woodkirk' in *Miscellanea* 10. *Thoresby Society* 33. 1935, pp. 22–60.

Selby

Collins, F., ed. *Selby wills*. Yorkshire Archaeological Society Record Series, 47. 1912.

South Cave

Kaner, Jennifer, et al, eds. *Goods and chattels, 1554–1642: wills, farm and household inventories from the parish of South Cave in the East Riding of Yorkshire*. University of Hull Centre for Continuing Education Development & Training, 1994.

Swaledale

Berry, Elizabeth K., ed. *Swaledale wills and inventories 1522–1600*. Yorkshire Archaeological Society record series, 152. 1998.

Temple Newsam

Kirk, G.E., ed. 'Wills, inventories, and bonds of the manor courts of Temple Newsam, 1612–1701', in *Miscellanea* 10. *Thoresby Society* 33. 1935, pp. 241–82.

Westerdale

Crossley, E.W., ed. 'The testamentary documents of Yorkshire peculiars', *Miscellanea II*. Yorkshire Archaeological Society Record Series 74. 1929, pp. 46–86. For Westerdale and Batley.

Whitby

Vickers, N. *A Yorkshire town in the eighteenth century: the probate inventories of Whitby, North Yorkshire, 1700–1800*. K.A.F. Brewin Books, 1986.

York

Cross, C., ed. *York clergy wills 1520–1600*. 2 vols. Borthwick texts and calendars 10 & 15. 1984–9. Pt. 1. Minster clergy. Pt. 2. City Clergy.

WALES

Glamorganshire

Riden, Philip, ed. *Glamorgan wills proved in the Prerogative Court of Canterbury 1392–1571: an interim calendar*. Cardiff, 1985.

Llewellyn, Howard P., ed. *Glamorgan wills proved in the Prerogative Court of Canterbury, 1601–1652*. M.A. Thesis, University of Wales (Cardiff), 1990.

Monmouthshire

Jones, Judith, ed. *Monmouthshire wills proved in the Prerogative Court of Canterbury 1560–1601*. South Wales Record Society, 12. 1997.

Morgan, Kathleen Frances Mary, ed. *Monmouthshire wills proved in the Prerogative Court of Canterbury 1602–1627*. MA thesis. University of Wales Cardiff, 1996.

SUMMARY LIST OF PRE-1858 PROBATE COURTS IN ENGLAND AND WALES

I t is important to be aware of all the courts that had probate jurisdiction in the area where you are researching. The list below will enable you to identify where wills could have been proved at a glance. It also indicates where their records are held. Where a court covered only a handful of parishes, I have tried to give details, although I make no claim for total accuracy. For more details, consult:

- Gibson, Jeremy, & Churchill, Else. *Probate jurisdictions: where to look for wills.* 5th ed. Federation of Family History Societies, 2002.

This is updated by:

- Recent Indexes to English, Welsh, Scottish and Irish Probate Records **www.dur.ac.uk/a.r.millard/genealogy/probate.php**

An increasing amount of detail concerning courts can be found at the

- National Wills Index **www.nationalwillsindex.com**

This site has pages related to many counties, which are not separately listed below. It may also be worth consulting the Familysearch Wiki, although at the time of writing the accuracy of its listing of probate courts leaves much to be desired:

- Probate Records in England **https://wiki.familysearch.org/en/ Category:Probate_records_in_England**

Details of the courts with national jurisdiction are not repeated in the individual county listings below, but should be assumed. The listing is by counties as they existed prior to the 1974 re-organization. I have also included references to some particularly useful websites.

National

Prerogative Court of Canterbury	TNA
High Court of Delegates	TNA
Court of Arches	Lambeth Palace Library
Prior (later, Dean & Chapter) of	
Christ Church, Canterbury	Canterbury Cathedral Library

(Had some jurisdiction during vacancies of the See of Canterbury)

Admiralty	TNA

(Had jurisdiction over the wills of Royal Navy seamen, 1786–1882)

Bedfordshire

Archdeaconry of Bedford	Bedfordshire Record Office
Biggleswade Peculiar	Bedfordshire Record Office
Leighton Buzzard Peculiar	Bedfordshire Record Office

Out-of-county courts with some Bedfordshire jurisdiction:

Lincoln Consistory Court	Lincolnshire Archives

(Superior Court of the Archdeaconry of Bedford)

Archdeaconry of Huntingdon	Huntingdonshire Archives

(Includes Everton)

Berkshire

Archdeaconry of Berkshire	Berkshire Record Office
Dean of Windsor Peculiar	St George's Chapel, Windsor
(Windsor Castle)	
Faringdon Peculiar	Berkshire Record Office
(Great Faringdon & Little Coxwell)	

Out-of-county courts with some Berkshire jurisdiction:

Consistory Court of Salisbury	Wiltshire and Swindon History Centre

(Superior Court of the Archdeaconry of Berkshire)

Dean of Salisbury Peculiars	Wiltshire and Swindon History Centre

(Arborfield, Blewbury with Aston Upthorpe, Hurst, Ruscombe, Sandhurst, Sonning, & Wokingham, etc)

Langford Peculiar	Oxfordshire Record Office

(Parish partially in Oxfordshire)

Wantage Peculiar	
(Dean & Canons of Windsor)	Wiltshire & Swindon History Centre

(Hungerford, West Ilsley, Shalbourne & Wantage)

Buckinghamshire

Archdeaconry of Buckingham	Centre for Buckinghamshire Studies
Aylesbury Peculiar	Centre for Buckinghamshire Studies

Bierton Peculiar   Bodleian Library, Oxford
Buckingham Peculiar   Centre for Buckinghamshire Studies
Monks Risborough Peculiar Centre for Buckinghamshire Studies
(Includes Monks Risborough & Halton)
Thame Peculiar   Oxfordshire History Centre
(Includes Aylesbury & Towersey)
Provost of Eton's Peculiar   Eton College

Out-of-county courts with some Buckinghamshire jurisdiction:

Consistory Court of Lincoln   Lincolnshire Archives
(Superior Court for Aylesbury & Buckingham Peculiars)
Archdeacon of St Albans Peculiars Hertfordshire Record Office
(Aston Abbots, Granborough, Little Horwood, & Winslow)
Consistory & Archdeaconry
    Courts of Oxford   Oxfordshire Record Office
(Included Caversfield, Ipstone, Lillingstone Lovell & Stokenchurch)

Cambridgeshire

Archdeaconry of Ely   Cambridgeshire Archives
Ely Consistory Court   Cambridgeshire Archives
Dean & Chapter of Ely Peculiar   Cambridgeshire Archives
Chancellor of the University
    of Cambridge   Cambridge University Library
Isleham and Freckenham Peculiar
    (of the Bishop of Rochester)   Suffolk Record Office
(Freckenham is in Suffolk)
King's College Peculiar   Kings College, Cambridge
Thorney Peculiar   Cambridgeshire Archives

Out-of-county courts with some Cambridgeshire jurisdiction:

Archdeaconry of Norfolk   Norfolk Record Office
(Included Outwell, Upwell, and Welsey)
Archdeaconry of Sudbury/
    Commissary Court of
    Bury St Edmunds   Suffolk Record Office
(Included Ashley cum Silverley, Burwell, Cheveley, Chippenham, Wood Ditton, Fordham, Kennett, Kirtling, Landwade, Newmarket All Saints, Snailwell, Soham, and Wicken)
Norwich Consistory Court   Norfolk Record Office
(Superior court for Archdeaconry of Norfolk)
Consistory Court of Rochester   Centre for Kentish Studies
(Superior court for Isleham & Freckenham Peculiar)

Cheshire
Consistory Court of Chester   Cheshire Archives & Local Studies

Out-of-county courts with some Cheshire jurisdiction:

Prerogative Court of York   Borthwick Institute
Chancery Court of York   Borthwick Institute

Cornwall
Archdeaconry of Cornwall   Cornwall Record Office
Deanery of St. Buryan Royal Peculiar Cornwall Record Office
(Included St Buryan, St Levan, and Sennen)

Out-of-county courts with some Cornish jurisdiction:

Consistory Court of Exeter   Destroyed
Dean & Chapter of Exeter
    peculiars   Destroyed
(Included St Agnes, Boconnock with Bradoc, Perranzabuloe, & St Winnow)

Cumberland
Consistory Court of Carlisle   Cumbria Record Office

Out-of-county courts with some Cumberland jurisdiction:

Commissary of the Archdeacon of
    Richmond (Western Deaneries)   Lancashire Record Office
(Included Copeland Deanery)
Consistory Court of Durham   Durham University Library
(Covered Alston, Garrigill, and – until c.1777 – Upper Denton)
Prerogative Court of York   Borthwick Institute
Chancery Court of York   Borthwick Institute

Derbyshire
There are no probate courts based in the county.
Burton upon Trent peculiar   Lichfield Record Office
(Included Branston, Burton upon Trent, Horninglow, Shobnall, Stapenhill,
Stretton, Wetmore & Yoxall)
Hartington peculiar   Lichfield Record Office
(Included Biggin, Buxton, Burbage, Hartington, High Needham, Newham,
Newhaven, Earl Sterndale, and Winster)
Manor of Dale Abbey Peculiar   Nottinghamshire Archives
Peak Forest Peculiar   Lichfield Record Office
Sawley Peculiar   Lichfield Record Office
(Included Breaston, Long Eaton, Risley, Sawley, and Wilne)

Out-of-county courts with some Derbyshire jurisdiction:

Consistory Court of Lichfield and
    Coventry   Lichfield Record Office
(Jurisdiction included much of Derbyshire)
Dean and Chapter of Lichfield
    Peculiar   Lichfield Record Office
(Included Ashford, Bakewell, Baslow, Beeley, Chapel-en-le-Frith, Chelmorton, Fairfield, Hope, Kniveton, Longston, Monyash, Peak Forest, Sheldon, Taddington, Tideswell, and Wormhill)

Devon

Many Devon probate records were destroyed when the Exeter Probate Registry was bombed in 1942. A comprehensive listing of surviving wills, both originals and transcripts, is being compiled. See:

- Wills and Probate Records: Locating Devon Wills and Administrations **www.devon.gov.uk/locating_wills_and_admin.htm#inland**

Principal Registry of Exeter Diocese	Destroyed
Consistory Court of Exeter	Destroyed
Archdeaconry of Barnstaple	Destroyed
Archdeaconry of Exeter	Destroyed
Archdeaconry of Totnes	Destroyed
Dean and Chapter of Exeter Peculiar	Destroyed
Prebend of Uffculme	Wiltshire and Swindon History Centre
Manor of Cockington Peculiar	Devon Record Office
Manor of Templeton Peculiar	No surviving records
Court of the Mayor of Exeter	Devon Record Office
Exeter Orphans Court	Devon Record Office
Custos and College of Vicars Choral in Exeter	Exeter Cathedral Library

(Included Woodbury – mostly destroyed)
Dean of Exeter's Peculiar   Destroyed

Out-of-county courts with some Devon jurisdiction:

Archdeaconry of Cornwall   Cornwall Record Office
(Included North Petherwin, St Giles in the Heath, and Werrington)
Archdeaconry of Dorset   Dorset History Centre
(Included Stockwood & Dalwood)

Dorset

Archdeaconry of Dorset	Dorset History Centre
Bristol Consistory Court (Dorset Division)	Dorset History Centre
(Superior court to the Archdeaconry of Dorset)	
Burton Bradstock Peculiar	Dorset History Centre
Canford Magna and Poole Peculiar	Dorset History Centre
Chardstock and Wambrook Prebend	Wiltshire and Swindon History Centre
Corfe Castle Peculiar	Dorset History Centre
Fordington Prebend	Wiltshire and Swindon History Centre
Manor and Liberty of Frampton	Dorset History Centre

(Included Bettiscombe, Bincombe, Compton Valence, Frampton, and Wintgerborne Came)

Gillingham Royal Peculiar	Wiltshire and Swindon History Centre
Lyme Regis and Halstock Prebend	Wiltshire and Swindon History Centre
Milton Abbas Peculiar	Dorset History Centre
(Includes Milton Abbas & Woolland)	
Netherbury Prebend	Wiltshire and Swindon History Centre
Preston and Sutton Poyntz Prebend	Wiltshire and Swindon History Centre
Sturminster Marshall Peculiar	Dorset History Centre

(Included Corfe Mullen, Hamworthy, Lytchet Minster, and Sturminster Marshall)

Wimborne Minster Peculiar	Dorset History Centre
Yetminster Prebend	Wiltshire and Swindon History Centre

Out-of-county courts with some Dorset jurisdiction:

Consistory Court of Salisbury	Wiltshire and Swindon History Centre
Dean of Salisbury's Peculiar	Wiltshire and Swindon History Centre
(Included 28 parishes scattered throughout the county)	
Dean and Chapter of Salisbury	Wiltshire and Swindon History Centre
(Included Stourpaine & Durweston)	

Durham

Consistory Court of Durham	Durham University Library

Out-of-county courts with some Durham jurisdiction:

Prerogative Court of York	Borthwick Institute
Chancery Court of York	Borthwick Institute

Essex

Archdeaconry of Essex	Essex Record Office
Archdeaconry of Colchester	Essex Record Office
Archdeaconry of Middlesex (Essex & Hertfordshire Division)	Essex Record Office
Commissary Court of London (Essex & Hertfordshire Division)	Essex Record Office
Good Easter Peculiar	Essex Record Office
Writtle with Roxwell Peculiar	Essex Record Office
Deanery of Bocking Peculiar	Essex Record Office

(Includes Bocking, Borley, Little Coggeshall, Latchingdon, Milton in Prittlewell, Runsell in Danbury, Southchurch, & Stisted)

Liberty of the Sokens	Essex Record Office

(Included Kirby-le-Soken, Thorpe-le-Soken, and Walton-le-Soken)

Havering-atte-Bower (or Hornchurch) Peculiar	New College Oxford

(Included Havering-atte-Bower, Hornchurch, & Romford)

Out-of-county courts with some Essex jurisdiction:

Consistory Court of London	London Metropolitan Archives

(Superior court for the Archdeaconries)

Commissary Court of London	Guildhall Library

(Included Chingford, Epping, Layton, Loughton, Nazeing, Waltham Holy Cross, Walthamstow and Woodford)

Dean and Chapter of Westminster Abbey Peculiar	Westminster City Archives Centre

(Included Newport, Creshall, Good Easter (also see this peculiar court), & Maldon St Mary)

Dean and Chapter of St Paul's Cathedral Peculiar	Guildhall Library

(Includes Barling, Belchamp St Pauls, Heybridge, Navestock, Tillingham, & Wickham St Pauls).

Gloucestershire and Bristol

Consistory Court of Gloucester	Gloucestershire Archives
Consistory Court of Bristol	Bristol Record Office
Bibury Peculiar	Gloucestershire Archives

(Included Aldsworth, Barnsley & Winson)

Bishop's Cleeve Peculiar	Gloucestershire Archives

(Included Bishops Cleeve and Stoke Orchard)

Withington Peculiar   Gloucestershire Archives
(Included Dowdeswell and Withington)
Mayor of Bristol's Orphans' Court   Bristol Record Office

Out-of-county courts with some Gloucestershire and Bristol jurisdiction:

Consistory Court of Bath
    and Wells   Somerset Record Office
(Included Bristol parishes of St Thomas, St Mary Radcliffe, Tempe or Holy
Cross – all destroyed in the bombing of Exeter)
Consistory Court of Hereford   Herefordshire Record Office
(Included twenty-eight parishes west of the Severn before 1541 only)

Hampshire

Consistory Court of Winchester	Hampshire Record Office
Archdeaconry of Winchester	Hampshire Record Office
Old Alresford with New Alresford and Medstead Peculiar	Hampshire Record Office
Alverstoke with Gosport Peculiar	Hampshire Record Office
Baughurst Peculiar	Hampshire Record Office
Binstead Peculiar (Isle of Wight)	Hampshire Record Office
Bishopstoke Peculiar	Hampshire Record Office
Bishops Waltham with Hamble and Bursledon Peculiar	Hampshire Record Office
Brighstone (Brixton) Peculiar, Isle of Wight	Hampshire Record Office
Burghclere Peculiar	Hampshire Record Office
Calbourne Peculiar	Hampshire Record Office
Cheriton with Kilmeston and Tichborne Peculiar	Hampshire Record Office
Chilbolton Peculiar	Hampshire Record Office
Chilcombe Peculiar	Hampshire Record Office
Compton Peculiar	Hampshire Record Office
Crawley with Hunton Peculiar	Hampshire Record Office
Droxford with Swanmore, Shidfield, Hill & Midlington Peculiar	Hampshire Record Office
Easton Peculiar	Hampshire Record Office
East Meon with Combe, Froxfield, Oxenbourne, Ramsdean and Steep Peculiar	Hampshire Record Office

(Includes Combe, East Meon, Steep, Froxfield, & the East Meon tythings
(parish-owned lands) of Oxenbourne and Ramsdean)

Exton Peculiar	Hampshire Record Office

Fareham with Catisfield and Dean Peculiar	Hampshire Record Office
Fawley with Exbury, Lepe, Cadlands, Ower, Holbury, Langley, Stanswood, Butsash, Hardley, Stone, Hythe and Brickmerston Peculiar	Hampshire Record Office
Hambledon with Denmead Peculiar	Hampshire Record Office
Hannington Peculiar	Hampshire Record Office
Havant with Leigh and Brockhampton Peculiar	Hampshire Record Office
Highclere Peculiar	Hampshire Record Office
Holdenhurst Peculiar	Hampshire Record Office
Houghton Peculiar	Hampshire Record Office
Hursley with Otterbourne, Merdon and Silkstead Peculiar	Hampshire Record Office
Hurstbourne Priors with St Mary Bourne Peculiar	Hampshire Record Office
Littleton Peculiar	Hampshire Record Office
Meonstoke with Soberton and Hoe Peculiar	Hampshire Record Office
Michelmersh with Braishfield Peculiar	Hampshire Record Office
Morestead Peculiar	Hampshire Record Office
North Baddesley Peculiar	Hampshire Record Office
North Waltham Peculiar	Hampshire Record Office
Overton with Tadley and Polhampton Peculiar	Hampshire Record Office
Ovington Peculiar	Hampshire Record Office
Ringwood with Harbridge Peculiar	Hampshire Record Office
St Faith or St Cross Peculiar	Hampshire Record Office
South Stoneham and St. Mary Extra with Allington and Shamblehurst Peculiar	Hampshire Record Office
Twyford with Owslebury and Brambridge Peculiar	Hampshire Record Office
Upham with Durley Peculiar	Hampshire Record Office
Warnford Peculiar	Hampshire Record Office
West Meon with Privett	Hampshire Record Office
Whitchurch with Freefolk and Charlecott Peculiar	Hampshire Record Office

Winnall Peculiar	Hampshire Record Office
Wonston with Sutton, Scotney and Cranborne Peculiar	Hampshire Record Office
East Woodhay with Ashmansworth Peculiar	Hampshire Record Office

Out-of-county courts with some Hampshire jurisdiction:

Archdeaconry of Berkshire (Included Stratfield Mortimer)	Berkshire Record Office
Archdeaconry of Surrey (Included Frensham)	London Metropolitan Archives
Dean and Chapter of Salisbury (Included Bramshaw)	Wiltshire and Swindon History Centre

Herefordshire

Consistory Court of Hereford	Herefordshire Record Office
Consistory Court of the Dean of Hereford	Herefordshire Record Office
(Included Hereford & 25 nearby parishes)	
Moreton Magna or Moreton on Lugg Peculiar	Herefordshire Record Office
Upper Bullinghope or Upper Bullingham Peculiar	Herefordshire Record Office
Little Hereford & Ashford Carbonell Peculiar	Herefordshire Record Office

Out-of-county courts with some Herefordshire jurisdiction:

Archdeaconry of Brecon   National Library of Wales
(Included Clodock, Dulas, Ffwddog Michaelchurch Excley, Ewyas Harold, Llancillo, St Margaret, Rowlston, & Waterstone)

Hertfordshire

Archdeaconry of St. Albans   Hertfordshire Record Office
(Included most of West and Central Hertfordshire)

Out-of-county courts with some Hertfordshire jurisdiction:

Consistory Court of London   London Metropolitan Archives
(Superior Court of the Archdeaconries of St Albans & Middlesex)
Archdeaconry of Middlesex   Essex Record Office
(Included thirty-one parishes in East Hertfordshire)

Commissary Court of London
(Essex and Herts division)   Essex Record Office
(Included Bishops Stortford, Little Hadham, Little Hormead, Much Hadham, and Royston)
Archdeaconry of Huntingdon
(Herts/Hitchen div.)   Hertfordshire Archives
(Included many parishes in South Hertfordshire and elsewhere)
Archdeaconry of Bedford   Bedfordshire Record Office
(Included Caddington & Studham)
Consistory Court of Lincoln   Lincolnshire Archive
(Superior court for Archdeaconries of Huntingdon & Bedford)
Dean and Chapter of St. Paul's
Cathedral   Guildhall Library
(Included Albury, Brent Pelham, Furneaux Pelham, and Navestock)

Huntingdonshire
Archdeaconry of Huntingdon
(Hitchin Division)   Huntingdonshire Archives
Brampton Peculiar   Huntingdonshire Archives
Buckden Peculiar   Huntingdonshire Archives
Leighton Bromswold Prebend   Huntingdonshire Archives
Stow Longa Prebend   Huntingdonshire Archives
(Includes Stow Longa, Easton, Spaldwick, Stow, Barham and Catworth Parva)

Out-of-county courts with some Huntingdonshire jurisdiction:

Consistory Court of Lincoln   Lincolnshire Archives
(Superior Court of the Archdeaconry of Huntingdon until 1837)
Dean and Chapter of Lincoln   Lincolnshire Archives
(Included Stow Longa and Leighton Bromswold)
Ely Consistory Court   Cambridge University Library
(Superior Court of the Archdeaconry of Huntingdon from 1837)
Consistory Court of Peterborough   Northamptonshire Record Office
(Included Washingley)
Archdeaconry Court of Bedford   Bedfordshire Record Office
(Included Tetworth)

Kent
Archdeaconry & Consistory
Courts of Canterbury   Centre for Kentish Studies
Archdeaconry & Consistory
Courts of Rochester   Centre for Kentish Studies

Dean of Peculiars (of the Arches,
   Croydon, & Shoreham)   Lambeth Palace Library
(the Deanery of Shoreham includes 38 parishes in W. Kent)
Rector of Cliffe   Centre for Kentish Studies
Provost of the College of
   Wingham   Centre for Kentish Studies
(Includes Wingham, Ash, Goodnestone, Nonington, and Womenswold, prior
to 1547)

Out-of-county courts with some Kentish jurisdiction:

Consistory Court of London   London Metropolitan Archives
(Included Charlton, Deptford, Eltham, Greenwich, Lee, Lewisham, Plumstead,
and Woolwich)

Lancashire
Halton Manor Peculiar   Borthwick Institute

Out-of-county courts with some Lancashire jurisdiction:

Consistory Court of Chester   Lancashire Record Office
(Included Lancashire south of the Ribble – the courts records have been
divided between Lancashire Record Office and Cheshire Archives)
Commissary of the Archdeaconry
   of Richmond (Western
   Deaneries)   Lancashire Record Office
(Included most of Lancashire north of the Ribble)
Dean and Chapter of York   Borthwick Institute
(Included Broughton, Kirkby Ireleth, & Seathwaite (Furness))
Archdeaconry of York   Borthwick Institute
(included Aighton, Bailey and Chaigley)
Prerogative Court of York   Borthwick Institute
Chancery Court of York   Borthwick Institute

Leicestershire
Archdeaconry of Leicester   Record Office for Leicestershire,
                                Leicester & Rutland
Manor of Evington Peculiar   Record Office for Leicestershire,
                                Leicester & Rutland
Groby Peculiar   Record Office for Leicestershire,
                                Leicester & Rutland
(Included Anstey, Bradgate Park and Hulgate, part of Charnwood Forest,
Cropston, Glenfield, Newtown Linford, Ratby, Stanton under Bardon, and
Swithland)
Old Dalby Peculiar   No known records

| Merevale Peculiar | Record Office for Leicestershire, Leicester & Rutland |
| Manor of Rothley | Record Office for Leicestershire, Leicester & Rutland |

(Included Barsby, South Croxton, Gaddesby, Grimston, Keyham, Mountsorrel, Rothley, Saxelby, part of Somerby, Wartnaby, Wycomb and Chadwell)

St. Margaret in Leicester Prebend   Record Office for Leicestershire, Leicester, and Rutland

(Included St. Margaret's Leicester, and the chapelry of Knighton)

Out-of-county courts with some Leicestershire jurisdiction:

Consistory Court of Lincoln   Lincolnshire Archives
(Superior court to Archdeaconry of Leicester)

Lincolnshire

Consistory Court of Lincoln	Lincolnshire Archives
Archdeaconry of Stow	Lincolnshire Archives
Dean and Chapter of Lincoln	Lincolnshire Archives

(Included twenty-five parishes scattered throughout the county)

Bishop Norton Prebend   Lincolnshire Archives
(Included Atterby, Bishop Norton, & Spital in the Street)

Caistor Prebend   Lincolnshire Archives
(Included Audleby, Clixby, Fonaby, Hundon and Holton le Moor)

Corringham Prebend   Lincolnshire Archives
(Included Aisby, Little Corringhan, Dunstall, Huckerby, Somerby and Yawthorpe)

Heydour Prebend   Lincolnshire Archives
(Included Heydour (or Haydor), Aisby, Culverthorpe, Kelby and Oasby)

Kirton in Lindsey Prebend   Lincolnshire Archives
Louth Prebend   Lincolnshire Archives
Sleaford Prebend   Lincolnshire Archives
(Included Holdingham, Old Sleaford, and Sleaford)

Stow in Lindsey Prebend   Lincolnshire Archives
(Included Bransby, Sturton, Normanby by Stow, & Stow in Lindsey)

Out-of-county courts with some Lincolnshire jurisdiction:

Prerogative Court of York   Borthwick Institute
Chancery Court of York   Borthwick Institute

London & Middlesex

Consistory Court of London   London Metropolitan Archives
(Superior court for the Diocese)

Court of Hustings	London Metropolitan Archives
(Covered the City of London)	
Archdeaconry of London	Guildhall Library

(Included forty-two City parishes, plus a few Middlesex parishes around Shoreditch and Clerkenwell)

Archdeaconry of Middlesex	London Metropolitan Archives
(Included twenty-six Middlesex parishes)	
Deanery of the Arches Peculiars	Lambeth Palace Library
(Included thirteen parishes in the City of London)	
Deanery of Croydon Peculiar	Lambeth Palace Library
(Included Harrow with Pinner, and Hayes with Norwood)	
Commissary Court of London	Guildhall Library
(Included fifty parishes in the City, and forty-four in Middlesex)	
Dean and Chapter of Westminster	
Peculiars	City of Westminster Archives

(Included Paddington, Precincts of the Abbey, St John the Evangelist, Westminster, St Margaret Westminster, St Martin in the Fields (part), precincts of St Martin le Grand, St Leonard, Foster Lane (part), and St Anne & St Agnes within Aldersgate (part))

Dean and Chapter of St Paul's	
Cathedral	Guildhall Library

(Included St Faith, St Giles Cripplegate, St Gregory, St Helen, and the Precinct of Portpool in the city; Chiswick, Friern Barnet, Precinct of Hoxton in Shoreditch, St Luke Old Street, St Pancras, Stoke Newington, and Willesden, Middlesex)

St Katherine's by the Tower	
Royal Peculiar	Guildhall Library

Norfolk

Consistory Court of Norwich	Norfolk Record Office
(Superior court for the Diocese)	
Archdeaconry of Norfolk	Norfolk Record Office
(Included much of South Norfolk)	
Archdeaconry of Norwich	Norfolk Record Office
(Included much of North Norfolk)	
Dean & Chapter of Norwich	
Peculiars	Norfolk Record Office

(Included the Precincts of Norwich Cathedral, Arminghall, Catton, Eaton, Hindolveston, Lakenham, Martham, Norwich St. Helen, Norwich St James, Norwich St Paul, Plumstead Magna, Sedgeford, Sprowston, Trowse and West Beckham)

Castle Rising Peculiar	Norfolk Record Office

(Included Castle Rising, Roydon, North Wootton, & South Wootton)

Great Cressingham Peculiar	Norfolk Record Office
Kings Lynn Borough Court	Kings Lynn Borough Archives
Court of the City of Norwich	Norfolk Record Office

Northamptonshire

Archdeaconry of Northampton	Northamptonshire Record Office
Consistory Court of Peterborough	Northamptonshire Record Office
Gretton Peculiar	Lincolnshire Archives

(Includes Gretton and Duddington)

Nassington Peculiar	Lincolnshire Archives

(Includes Nassington, Apethorpe, Woodnewton and Yarnwell)

Out-of-county courts with some Northamptonshire jurisdiction:

Dean and Chapter of Lincoln	Lincolnshire Archives
Banbury Peculiar	Oxfordshire History Centre

(Includes Kings Sutton & Grimsbury)

Northumberland

Hexham & Hexhamshire Peculiar	Borthwick Institute

(Included Allendale, West Allen, Hexham, Nine Banks, St John Lee, St Oswald, St Mary Bingfield, and Whitley)

Thockrington Prebend	Borthwick Institute

Out-of-county courts with some Northumberland jurisdiction:

Consistory Court of Durham	Durham University Library

(Included most of Northumberland)

Prerogative Court of York	Borthwick Institute
Chancery Court of York	Borthwick Institute

Nottinghamshire

Archdeaconry of Nottingham	Nottinghamshire Archives
Apesthorpe Prebend	Borthwick Institute
Bole Prebend	Borthwick Institute
Manor of Edwinstowe	Nottinghamshire Archives

(Included Edwinstowe and Carburton)

Manor of Gringley-on-the-Hill or Bawtry	Nottinghamshire Archives

(Included Gringley-on-the-Hill &, after about 1800, Misterton, West Stockwith, Walkeringham and Beckingham)

Kinoulton Peculiar	Nottinghamshire Archives
Manor of Mansfield	Nottinghamshire Archives

(Included Mansfield, Mansfield Woodhouse, Sutton-in-Ashfield, Hucknall-under-Huthwaite, Budby, Kilton and Scofto in Worksop, part of Worksop)

Manor of Rufford Abbey   Nottinghamshire Archives
Manor of St John of Jerusalem
   or Shelford St Johns   Nottinghamshire Archives
(Included Aslockton, Car Colston, Carlton-in-Gedling, Cotgrave, Flintham, Hickling, Radcliffe-on-Trent, Scarrington and Willoughby-on-the-Wolds)
Manor of Skegby and Teversal   Nottinghamshire Archives
Southwell Peculiar   Nottinghamshire Archives
(Included twenty-eight parishes in mid-Nottinghamshire)

Out-of-county courts with some Nottinghamshire jurisdiction:

Prerogative Court of York   Borthwick Institute
Chancery Court of York   Borthwick Institute
Dean & Chapter of York   Borthwick Insititute
(Included Askham, East Drayton, Laneham, Misterton, Stokeham, West Stockwith, & Treswell)

Oxfordshire
Archdeaconry of Oxford   Oxfordshire History Centre
Consistory Court of Oxford   Oxfordshire History Centre
Banbury Peculiar   Bodleian Library, Oxford
Langford Peculiar   Oxfordshire History Centre
(Included Langford and Little Faringdon)
Dorchester Peculiar   Oxfordshire History Centre
(Included Dorchester, Benson, Chiselhampton, Clifton Hampden, Drayton St Leonard, Marsh Baldon, Nettlebed, Pishill, Stadhampton, Toot Baldon, & Warborough)
Thame Peculiar   Oxfordshire History Centre
(Includes Great Milton, Sydenham, Tetsworth & Thame)
Manor of Sibford   Oxfordshire History Centre
Court of the Chancellor of the
   University of Oxford   Oxford University Archives

Out-of-county courts with some Oxfordshire jurisdiction:

Monks Risborough Peculiar   Centre for Buckinghamshire Studies
(Includes Newington with Britwell Prior in Oxfordshire)

Rutland
Caldecote Prebend   Record Office for Leicestershire,
                           Leicester & Rutland
Empingham Peculiar   Lincolnshire Archives
(Includes Harwick)

146

Ketton with Tixover Prebend   Record Office for Leicestershire,
             Leicester & Rutland
Liddington Prebend   Record Office for Leicestershire,
             Leicester & Rutland
(Included Caldecott, Lidington, and Thorpe by Water in Seaton parish)

Out-of-county courts with some Rutland jurisdiction:

Consistory Court of Peterborough Northamptonshire Record Office
Archdeaconry of Northampton Northamptonshire Record Office
(Included most of Rutland)

Shropshire
Ashford Carbonell Peculiar   Herefordshire Record Office
Bridgnorth Royal Peculiar   Lichfield Record Office
(Includes Alveley, Bobbington, Bridgenorth St Mary, Bridgenorth St Leonard, Claverley, & Quatford)
Manor of Ellesmere   Lichfield Record Office
(Includes Ellesmere, with Colemere and Lyneal, & Welshampton)
Manor of Longdon on Tern   Shropshire Archives
Ludlow Corporation   Shropshire Archives
Prees or Pipe Minor Prebend Lichfield Record Office
Manor of Ruyton-of-the-Eleven-
 Towns   Shropshire Archives
St Mary Shrewsbury Royal
 Peculiar   Lichfield Record Office
(Includes Albrighton, Astley, Clive, & St Mary Shrewsbury)
Wombridge Abbey Peculiar   Shropshire Archives

Out-of-county courts with some Shropshire jurisdiction:

Consistory Court of Hereford Herefordshire Record Office
(Covered most of SW Shropshire)
Consistory Court of Lichfield
 & Coventry   Lichfield Record Office
(Covered most of NE Shropshire)
Consistory Court of St. Asaph National Library of Wales
(Included Kinnerley, Knockin, Llanyblodwell, Llanymynech, Melverley, Oswestry, St. Martin's, Selattyn and Whittington)
Consistory Court of Worcester Worcestershire History Centre
(Included Halesowen)
Manor of Pattingham
 (Staffordshire)   Lichfield Record Office
(included Township of Rudge, Shropshire)

Somerset

Many Somerset wills were lost in the war-time bombing of the Exeter probate registry. For a discussion of surviving records, see:

- Wills **www1.somerset.gov.uk/archives/Wills.htm**

Copies of wills sent to the Estate Duty Office are now held by Somerset Record Office.

Consistory Court of the Archdeaconry of Wells	Somerset Record Office (mostly destroyed)
Consistory Court of the Archdeaconry of Taunton	Somerset Record Office (mostly destroyed)
Consistory Court of the Dean of Wells	Somerset Record Office (mostly destroyed)
Consistory Court of the Dean & Chapter of Wells	Somerset Record Office (mostly destroyed)
Consistory Court of Bath & Wells	Somerset Record Office (mostly destroyed)
Consistory Court of Bristol (Deanery of Bristol) (Included Abbots Leigh)	Bristol Record Office
Banwell Peculiar	Destroyed
Churchill Peculiar	Destroyed
Ilminster Peculiar	Destroyed
Kingsbury with East Lambrook Peculiar	Destroyed
North Wooton Peculiar	Destroyed
Pilton Peculiar	Destroyed
Witham Friary Peculiar	Destroyed
Ashill Prebend	Destroyed
Buckland Dinham Prebend	Destroyed
Compton Bishop Prebend	Destroyed
Compton Dundon Prebend	Destroyed
Cudworth & Knowle Prebend	Destroyed
Easton-in-Gordano Prebend	Destroyed
East Harptree Prebend	Destroyed
Haselbury Plucknett Prebend	Destroyed
Henstridge Prebend	Destroyed
Ilminster Royal Peculiar	Destroyed
Ilton Prebend	Destroyed
Litton Prebend	Destroyed
St. Decumans Prebend	Destroyed
Timberscombe Prebend	Destroyed

West Lydford Prebend	Destroyed
Whitelackington Prebend	Destroyed
Wiveliscombe with Fitzhead Prebend	Destroyed
Wookey Prebend	Destroyed
Yatton & Kenn Prebend	Destroyed

Out-of-county courts with some Somerset jurisdiction:

Fordington Prebend (Dorset)   Wiltshire & Swindon History Centre
(Included Writhlington, Somerset)

Staffordshire

Consistory Court of Lichfield
   and Coventry   Lichfield Record Office
Dean & Chapter of Lichfield   Lichfield Record Office
(Included Cannock, Farewell, Harborne, The Close Lichfield, Regeley and Smethwick)
Dean of Lichfield   Lichfield Record Office
(Included Lichfield Cathedral, the Lichfield parishes of Christ Church, St Chad, St Mary & St Michael; with surrounding parishes of Adbaston, Brewood, Hammerwich, Haselour, Stafford, Streethay, Wall and Whittington)
Alrewas and Weeford Peculiar   Lichfield Record Office
(Included Alrewas, Blithbury, Edingale, Fradley, Hints, King's Bromley (Regis Bromley), Mavesyn Ridware, Pipe Ridware, Packington, Swinfen and Weeford)
Burton on Trent Peculiar   Lichfield Record Office
Colwich Peculiar   Lichfield Record Office
(Included Colton, Colwich, Fradswell, Great Haywood, and Shugborough)
Eccleshall Peculiar   Lichfield Record Office
(Included Broughton, Charnes, Coates, Eccleshall, Fairoaks, Slindon, Sugnall, Walton and Wetwood)
Manor of Gnosall   Lichfield Record Office
Hansacre and Armitage Peculiar   Lichfield Record Office
(Included Armitage, Brownhills, Hansacre, Hints, Norton Canes, Ogle Hay and Wyrley)
High Offley and Flixton
   (Lancashire) Peculiar   Lichfield Record Office
Longdon Peculiar   Lichfield Record Office
(Included Longdon and Bloxwich)
Manor of Pattingham Peculiar   Lichfield Record Office

Penkridge Peculiar   Lichfield Record Office
(Included Congreve, Coppenhall, Dunston, Levedale, Penkridge, Rodbaston, Saredon, Shareshill, Stretton and Water Eaton)
Prebend of Prees or Pipe Minor
    Peculiar   Lichfield Record Office
(Included Calverhall, Darlaston, Prees, Stafford St Chad, Tipton, Whixhall and Willaston)
Manor of Sedgley Peculiar   Dudley Archives & Local History Service
Stafford Collegiate Church   William Salt Library
(Jurisdiction wide but uncertain)
Tettenhall Peculiar   Lichfield Record Office
(Included Bilbrook, Codsall, Compton, Kingswinford, Kingswood, Oaken, Perton, Teetenhall, Trescott, The Wergs and Wrottesley)
Manor of Tyrley   Lichfield Record Office
(Included, Almington, Bloore-with-Tyrley, Hales, & Market Drayton)
Whittington and Baswich
    Peculiar   Lichfield Record Office
(Included Acton Trussel, Bednal, Baswich and Whittington)
Wolverhampton Peculiar   Lichfield Record Office
(Included Bentley, Bilston, Bushbury, Hatherton, Hilton, Kinvaston, Pelsall, Wolverhampton Parish, Willenhall and Wednesfield)

Suffolk

Archdeaconry of Suffolk   Ipswich & East Suffolk Record Office
(Covered East Suffolk)
Archdeaconry of Sudbury   Suffolk Record Office Bury St Edmunds
(Covered West Suffolk; incorporated Commissary Court for Bury St Edmunds)

Out-of-county courts with some Suffolk jurisdiction:

Consistory Court of Norwich   Norfolk Record Office
(Superior court for Suffolk Archdeaconries)
Archdeaconry of Norfolk   Norfolk Record Office
(Includes Rushford)
Archdeaconry of Norwich   Norfolk Record Office
(Includes Bramford, Thetford, & Great Finborough)
Consistory Court of Ely   Cambridge University Library
(Superior court for Sudbury Archdeaconry post 1837)
Deanery of Bocking (Essex)
    Peculiar   Essex Record Office
(Includes Monks Edleigh, Hadleigh & Moulton)
Isleham (Cambridgeshire) and
    Freckenham Peculiar   Suffolk Record Office Bury St Edmunds

Surrey

Archdeaconry of Surrey   London Metropolitan Archives

Out-of-county courts with some Surrey jurisdiction:

Commissary Court of Winchester,
     Archdeaconry of Surrey   London Metropolitan Archives
Consistory Court of Winchester   Hampshire Record Office
Consistory Court of Bishop
     of London   London Metropolitan Archives
(Included South London parishes transferred to the Diocese of London in 1846)
Consistory Court of Canterbury   Kent Archive Service
(From 1837, included Addington and Lambeth)
Deanery of Croydon   Lambeth Palace Library
(Included Barnes, Burstow, Charlwood, Cheam, Church Newington, Croydon, East Horsley, Merstham, Mortlake, Putney, Roehampton, Walworth St Peter, & Wimbledon)

Sussex

Archdeaconry of Chichester   West Sussex Record Office
Archdeaconry of Lewes   East Sussex Record Office
Dean of Chichester   West Sussex Record Office
(Included Chichester St Andrew, Chichester St Bartholomew, Chichester St Martin, Chichester St Olave, Chichester St Peter the Great, Chichester St Peter the Less, Chichester St Pancras, New Fishbourne, & Rumboldswyke)
Deaneries of Pagham and Tarring   West Sussex Record Office
(Included Chichester All Saints, Horsham (part), East Lavant, Pagham, Patching, Slindon, South Bersted, Tangmere, & West Tarring with Durrington & Heen)
Deanery of South Malling   East Sussex Record Office
(Included The Cliffe or St Thomas Lewes, Edburton, Framfield, Glynde, Isfield, Lindfield, Mayfield, Ringmer, South Malling, Stanmer, Uckfield, & Wadhurst)
Battle Peculiar   East Sussex Record Office

Out-of-county courts with some Sussex jurisdiction:

Archdeaconry & Consistory
     Courts of Rochester   Centre for Kentish Studies
Included Lamberhurst (partly in Kent)

Warwickshire

Manor of Baddesley-Clinton   Warwickshire Record Office
Manor of Barston   Warwickshire Record Office

Manor of Bishop's Itchington	Lichfield Record Office
(Included Chadshunt and Gaydon)	
Bishops Tachbrook Peculiar	Lichfield Record Office
Prebend of Hampton-Lucy	Shakespeare Birthplace Trust
(Included Hampton-Lucy, Alveston, Wasperton & Chilcote)	
Manor of Knowle	Warwickshire Record Office
Manor of Merevale	Lichfield Record Office
Manor of Packwood	Warwickshire Record Office
Manor of Tachbrook	Lichfield Record Office
Manor of Temple Balsall	Warwickshire Record Office
Prebend of Ufton	Lichfield Record Office
Stratford-upon-Avon Peculiar	Shakespeare Birthplace Trust

Out-of-county courts with some Warwickshire jurisdiction:

Consistory Court of Lichfield	Lichfield Record Office
(Covered most of North & West Warwickshire)	
Consistory Court of Worcester	Worcestershire Record Office
(Covered much of South Warwickshire)	
Consistory Court of Gloucester	Gloucestershire Record Office
(Included Welford and Sutton-Under-Brailes)	
Dean and Chapter of Lichfield	Lichfield Record Office
(Included Arley and Edgbaston)	
Banbury & Cropredy Peculiar	
Oxfordshire	Oxfordshire Record Office
(Included Mollington – partly in Warwickshire)	

Westmorland

Consistory Court of Carlisle	Cumbria Record Office
(Covered N.E. Westmorland)	
Manor of Docker	Cumbria Record Office
Manor of Ravenstonedale	Cumbria Record Office
Manor of Temple Sowerby	Cumbria Record Office

Out-of-county courts with some Westmorland jurisdiction:
Commissary of the Archdeaconry
   of Richmond (Western Deaneries) Lancashire Record Office
(Covered S.W. Westmorland)

Wiltshire

| Consistory Court of Salisbury | Wiltshire & Swindon History Centre |

(Superior court for the diocese; also bishop's peculiars of Berwick St. James, Devizes St. John and St. Mary, West Lavington, Marlborough St. Mary and St. Peter, Preshute, Potterne, Stert, and Trowbridge with Staverton)

Archdeaconry of Salisbury   Wiltshire & Swindon History Centre
(Covers much of S.Wiltshire)
Archdeaconry of Wiltshire   Wiltshire & Swindon History Centre
(Covers much of N.Wiltshire)
Archdeaconry of the Sub-Dean
   of Salisbury   Wiltshire & Swindon History Centre
(Included Salisbury parishes of St Edmund, St Martin and Thomas; also
Milford and Stratford-sub-Castle)
Dean of Salisbury   Wiltshire & Swindon History Centre
(Included Baydon, Heytesbury, Hill Deverill, Horningsham, Knook, Mere,
Ramsbury, Salisbury Close, & Swallowcliffe)
Dean and Chapter of Salisbury   Wiltshire & Swindon History Centre
(Included Bishops Cannings with Southbroom, Britford, & Homington)
Precentor of Salisbury   Wiltshire & Swindon History Centre
(Included Westbury with Bratton & Dilton)
Prebend of Bishopstone   Wiltshire & Swindon History Centre
Prebend of Calne   Wiltshire & Swindon History Centre
(Included Alderbury, Farley, Pitton, Berwick Bassett, Blackland, Cherhill &
Figheildean)
Castle Combe Peculiar   Wiltshire & Swindon History Centre
Prebend of Chute and Chisenbury   Wiltshire & Swindon History Centre
(Included Chute, Chisenbury, & Winterbourne Dauntsey)
Prebend of Coombe Bissett
   and Harnham   Wiltshire & Swindon History Centre
Perpetual Vicarage of Corsham   Wiltshire & Swindon History Centre
Prebend of Durnford   Wiltshire & Swindon History Centre
Prebend of Highworth   Wiltshire & Swindon History Centre
(Included Highworth, South Marston, Sevenhampton, & Broad Blunsden)
Prebend of Netheravon   Wiltshire & Swindon History Centre
Salisbury Corporation   Wiltshire & Swindon History Centre
Lord Warden of Savernake Forest   Wiltshire & Swindon History Centre
(Included Great and Little Bedwyn, & Collingbourne Ducis)
Prebend of Wilsford and
   Woodford   Wiltshire & Swindon History Centre

Out-of-county courts with some Wiltshire jurisdiction:

Consistory Court of Winchester   Hampshire Record Office
(Included Whitsbury & West Wellow)
Consistory Court of Gloucester   Gloucestershire Archives
(Included Kingswood & Marston Meysey)
Dean & Canons of Windsor
   in Wantage   Wiltshire & Swindon History Centre
(Included Ogbourne St Andrew, Ogbourne St George, & Shalbourne)

Prebend of Hurstbourne
  (Hampshire) and Burbage
  (Wiltshire)   Wiltshire & Swindon History Centre

Worcestershire
Consistory Court of Worcester   Worcestershire History Centre
Court of the Dean and Chapter
  of Worcester   Worcestershire History Centre
(Included Barrow, the College precincts in Worcester, Kempsey, Norton near
Kempsey, St. Michael in Bedwardine, Stoulton, Tibberton, & Wolverley)
Evesham Peculiar   Worcestershire Historty Centre
Rector of Alvechurch or Allchurch Worcestershire Historty Centre
Rector of Bredon with Norton
  and Cutsdean   Worcestershire History Centre
Rector of Fladbury   Worcestershire History Centre
Hanbury Peculiar   Worcestershire History Centre
Hartlebury Peculiar   Worcestershire History Centre
Rector of Ripple with Queenhill
  and Holdfast   Worcestershire History Centre
Rector of Tredington with
  Shipston upon Stour   Worcestershire History Centre

Out-of-county courts with some Worcestershire jurisdiction:

Consistory Court of Hereford   Herefordshire Record Office
(Includes twenty Worcestershire parishes)

Yorkshire
For details of records held by the Borthwick Institute of Historical Research,
see:

- Probate Records **www.york.ac.uk/media/library/documents/
  borthwick/3.1.1.20guidfeprob.pdf**

  Probate records at the West Yorkshire Archive Service Leeds are listed by

- Collections Guide 4 **www.archives.wyjs.org.uk/documents/archives/
  Collections%20Guide%204.pdf**

Prerogative Court of York   Borthwick Institute
(Superior court for the Province of York)
Chancery Court of the
  Archbishop of York   Borthwick Institute
(Appeal court)

Consistory Court of the
    Archbishop of York   Borthwick Institute
(Jurisdiction over clergy, and over peculiars during visitations and inhibitions)
Exchequer Court of the
    Archbishop of York   Borthwick Institute
(Jurisdiction over the Diocese of York, except peculiars)
Dean and Chapter of York   Borthwick Institute
(Exercised jurisdiction during vacancies in the See; also had peculiars in many parishes in York, and in each Riding)
Chancellor of York   Borthwick Institute
(Included Acklam near Malton, North and South Anston, Firbeck, Handsworth, Laughton en le Morthen, Letwell with Gildingwells, Thorpe Salvin, Throapham, St John, Wales, & Wawne)
Commissary Court of the
    Archdeaconry of Richmond,
    Eastern Deaneries   Leeds District Archives
(Covered Deaneries of Boroughbridge, Catterick, and Richmond, other than peculiars)
Dean of York's Peculiar   Borthwick Institute
(Included Allerston, Allerthorpe, Barnby Moor, Bielby, Ebberston, Ellerburn, Fangfoss, Great Givendale, Goathland, Hayton, Kilham, Kildwick Percy, Meltonby, Millington, Newton, Pickering, Pocklington, Thornton on Spalding Moor, Wilton, and Yapham)
Precentor of York   Borthwick Institute
(Included Great Driffield, Little Driffield, Haxby (part), & Little Ouseburn)

East Riding, York, and the Ainsty
Acomb Peculiar   Borthwick Institute
Manor of Askham Bryan   Borthwick Institute
Prebend of Barmby Moor   Borthwick Institute
Manor of Beeford   Borthwick Institute
Provost of the Collegiate
    Church of St John, Beverley Borthwick Institute
(Included twenty-two parishes around Beverley)
Prebend of Bilton   Borthwick Institute
Bishop Wilton Peculiar   Borthwick Institute
Dunnington Peculiar   Borthwick Institute
Prebend of Fridaythorpe   Borthwick Institute
Prebend of Givendale   Borthwick Institute
(included Givendale & Millington)
Prebend of Grindal   Borthwick Institute
Prebend of Holme   Borthwick Institute
(Included Withernwick)

Kingston upon Hull Corporation   Hull History Centre
Prebend of Langtoft   Borthwick Institute
(Included Langtoft, Cottam, & North Grimston)
Mappleton   Borthwick Institute
(Peculiar of the Archdeacon of the East Riding)
Prebend of Market Weighton   Borthwick Institute
(Included Market Weighton and Shipton)
Prebend of North Newbald   Borthwick Institute
(Included North & South Newbald)
Preston in Holderness   Borthwick Institute
(Peculiar of the Sub-Dean of York)
Prebend of Riccall   Borthwick Institute
Prebend of South Cave   Borthwick Institute
Tunstall Peculiar   Borthwick Institute
St Leonard's Hospital, York   York Minster Library
(Included Carneby, North and South Cave, Hotham, Nunburnholme, Burniston, Kirkby, Newton-on-Ouse, Over Helmsley, Pickhill, Topcliffe, Gisburn, Rufforth, Saxton, All Saints North Street, St. Helen's Stonegate, St. Giles' Gillygate, and St. Lawrence in the city of York)

North Riding
Aldbrough Peculiar   York Minster Library
(In Stanwick St John)
Alne and Tollerton Peculiar of
   the Bishop of Durham   Borthwick Institute
(Included Alne, Skelton, Tollerton, & Wigginton)
Allerton and Allertonshire
   Peculiar   Durham University Library
(Included Northallerton, & chapelries of Deighton, Brompton and Worsall, with Kirkby Sigston and West Rounton)
Prebend of Ampleforth   Borthwick Institute
(Included Ampleforth & Heslington)
Manor of Arkengarthdale with
   New Forest and Hope   Leeds District Archives
Prebend of Bugthorpe   Borthwick Institute
Craike Peculiar of the Bishop
   of Durham   Durham University Library
Dean and Chapter of Durham's
   Peculiar in Howden and
   Howdenshire   Borthwick Institute
(Included Asselby, Barlby, Barnby Marsh, Blacktoft, Brantingham, Eastrington, Ellerker, Hemingbrough, Holtby, Howden, Laxton, Skipwith, Walkington, & Welton)

Prebend of Husthwaite   Borthwick Institute
(Included Husthwaite & Carlton Husthwaite)
Manor of Linton on Ouse   Borthwick Institute
Prebend of Masham   Leeds District Archives
(Included Kirkby Malzeard and Masham, with chapelries of Hartwith, Winsley and Middlesmoor)
Deanery & Royal Peculiar of
    the Collegiate Church of
    Middleham   Leeds District Archives
Manor of Newton-on-Ouse
    with Beningborough   Borthwick Institute
Prebend of Osbaldwick   (mostly destroyed)Borthwick Institute
(Included Osbaldwick (part), Gate Helmsley, & Murton (part))
Prebend of Salton   (mostly destroyed)Borthwick Institute
Prebend of Stillington   (mostly destroyed)Borthwick Institute
Prebend of Strensall   (mostly destroyed)Borthwick Institute
(Included Strensall, Haxby (part), Murton (part), & Osbaldwick (part))
Prebend of Warthill   (mostly destroyed)Borthwick Institute

West Riding
Manor of Altofts in Normanton   Leeds District Archives
Manor of Barnoldswick   Borthwick Institute
Manor of Batley   Bradford Central Library
Manors of Crossley, Bingley,
    Cottingley and Pudsey   Borthwick Institute
Prebend of Fenton   Borthwick Institute
(Included Church Fenton, Micklefield, & Sherburn in Elmet)
Manor of Hunsingore   Leeds District Archives
(Included Hunsingore, Great Ribston cum Walshford & Cattal)
Honour of Knaresborough   Leeds District Archives
(Included Burton Leonard, Farnham, Fewston, Great Ouseburn, Hamps-thwaite, Knaresborough, Pannal, South Stainley with Cayton, and Staveley, plus many townships)
Prebend of Knaresborough   Borthwick Institute
(Covered parts of Knaresborough)
Leeds Kirkgate Peculiar   Leeds District Archives
Manor of Marsden   Borthwick Institute
Mexborough & Ravenfield
    Peculiar   Borthwick Institute
(Peculiar of the Archdeacon of York)
Selby Peculiar   Borthwick Institute
(Included Selby, Barlow, Brayton, Burn, Gateforth, Hambleton, & Thorpe Willoughby)

Manor of Silsden	Borthwick Institute
Snaith Peculiar	Borthwick Institute

(Included Airmyn, Balne, Carlton, Cowick, Goole, Gowdall, Heck, Hensall, Hook, Ousefleet, Pollington, Rawcliffe, Reedness, Snaith, Swinefleet, & Whitgift)

Manor of Temple Newsam	Borthwick Institute
Prebend of Ulleskelf	Borthwick Institute
Wadworth Peculiar	Borthwick Institute
Manor of Warmfield with Heath	Leeds District Archives
Prebend of Wetwang	Borthwick Institute

(Included Elloughton, Fimber, Fridaythorpe, Kirkby Wharfe, Ulleskelf and Wetwang)

Whitkirk Peculiar	Leeds District Archives
Prebend of Wistow	Borthwick Institute

(Included Cawood, Monk Fryston and Wistow)

Out-of-county courts with some Yorkshire jurisdiction:

Commissary of the Archdeaconry of Richmond	Western Deaneries Lancashire Record Office

(Included Bentham, Clapham, Sedbergh & Thonton in Lonsdale)

Consistory Court of Chester	Lancashire Record Office

(Included chapelries of Saddleworth & Whitewell)

Archdeaconry of Nottingham	Nottinghamshire Archives

(Included Rossington, Blyth & Finningley)

WALES

Anglesey
Out-of-county court with Anglesey jurisdiction:

Court of the Bishop of Bangor	National Library of Wales

Breconshire

Archdeaconry of Brecon	National Library of Wales

Caernarvonshire

Consistory Court of Bangor	National Library of Wales

Cardiganshire
Out-of-county court with Cardiganshire jurisdiction:

Consistory Court of St David	National Library of Wales

158

Carmarthenshire
Out-of-county court with Carmarthenshire jurisdiction:

Consistory Court of St David   National Library of Wales

Denbighshire
Out-of-county courts with some Denbighshire jurisdiction:

Consistory Court of St Asaph   National Library of Wales
(Includes East and West Denbighshire)
Consistory Court of Bangor   National Library of Wales
(Includes Mid-Denbighshire)
Consistory Court of Chester   National Library of Wales
(Included Holt)

Flintshire
Consistory Court of St. Asaph   National Library of Wales
Consistory Court of Chester   National Library of Wales
Hawarden Peculiar   National Library of Wales

Glamorganshire
Consistory Court of Llandaff   National Library of Wales
Consistory Court of St David   National Library of Wales
(Included parishes in the far west of Glamorganshire)

Merionethshire
Out-of-county courts with some Merionethshire jurisdiction:

Consistory Court of St Asaph   National Library of Wales
(Included East Merionethshire)
Consistory Court of Bangor   National Library of Wales
(Included West Merionethshire)

Monmouthshire
Consistory Court of Llandaff   National Library of Wales

Out-of-county courts with some Monmouthshire jurisdiction:

Consistory Consistory Court
   of Hereford   Herefordshire Record Office
(Included Monmouth)
Archdeaconry of Brecon   National Library of Wales
(Included Cwmyoy, Llanthony, and Oldcastle)

Montgomeryshire

Consistory Court of St Asaph   National Library of Wales

Out-of-county courts with some Montgomeryshire jurisdiction:

Consistory Court of Bangor   National Library of Wales
(Included Carno, Llandinam, Llangurig, Llanidloes, Llanwynog, Penstrowed and Trefeglwys)
Consistory Court of St David   National Library of Wales
(Included Kerry and Mochdre)
Consistory Court of Hereford   Herefordshire Record Office
(Included Forden, Mainstone, Montgomery, Snead and Worthen)

Pembrokeshire

Consistory Court of St David   National Library of Wales

Radnorshire

Archdeaconry of Brecon   National Library of Wales
Consistory Court of Hereford   Herefordshire Record Office
(Included Discoed, Knighton, Michaelchurch on Arrow, Norton, Presteigne, and Old and New Radnor)

Appendix 2

HANDWRITING AND LATIN

With the passing of the centuries, both styles of handwriting, and the language used, change. Consequently, the difficulty in understanding what is written increases. The handwriting of sixteenth- and seventeenth-century England is quite different from modern handwriting. Even if English is used in wills of this date, some of the terms used in them are obsolete or obscure. Before the mid-sixteenth century, scribes frequently wrote in Latin; its use was only abolished in 1733.

It is not difficult to read seventeenth-century handwriting. All that is required is practice, patience, and persistence. Always remember that what you are trying to read was meant to be read. It is frequently a matter of knowing what to expect, and of comparing difficult letters with those used elsewhere in the document you are reading. Latin documents are more difficult. It is not only the unfamiliarity of the language used, but also the frequently heavy use of abbreviations, and the fact that scribes were not necessarily good latinists themselves – their grammar sometimes leaves much to be desired.

The National Archives have produced a number of online tutorials which will help you to read old wills. These include a basic introduction to palaeography, two tutorials on Latin, and a guide to Latin palaeography. These are free:

- The National Archives: Reading Old Documents
  www.nationalarchives.gov.uk/records/reading-old-documents.htm

There are also many published guides to old handwriting; the best is:

- Marshall, Hilary. *Palaeography for Family and Local Historians.* Phillimore, 2004.

See also:

- Hoskin, P.M., Slinn, S.L., & Webb, C.C. *Reading the Past: Sixteenth and Seventeenth Century English Handwriting.* York; Borthwick Institute, 2001.

Letter forms are illustrated in:

- Buck, W.S.B. *Examples of English handwriting 1550–1650.* Phillimore for the Society of Genealogists, 1965.

The English used in the seventeenth century and earlier included many words which are now obsolete. A useful dictionary of such words is provided by:

- Raymond, Stuart A. *Words from wills and other probate records 1500–1800: a glossary.* Federation of Family History Societies, 2004.

Spelling was not uniform in this period; you will frequently find 'y' substituted for 'I', or '-tion' endings replaced by '-con'. If at first you do not understand a word, try pronouncing it: you will quickly realise that 'qwysshons', for example, are actually cushions. Sometimes words run into one another, as they still do in German. 'Shalbe', for example, is 'shall be', and 'thappurtenances' is 'the appurtenances'. You will also come across relics of the 'thorn' (represented as 'y') that once formed part of the Anglo-Saxon alphabet, but is now obsolete. Do not allow this to give rise to false archaisms such as 'ye', when what was intended was 'the'.

Latin is more difficult. However, it can be learnt. The Latin used in the sixteenth and seventeenth century does differ from classical Latin. In Latin wills and other documents that family historians are likely to use, terms (some of which are listed in Appendix 4) are sometimes used repetitively, and consequently become easy to recognize with practice. The best introduction is:

- Stuart, Denis. *Latin for local and family historians: a beginners guide.* Phillimore, 1995.

See also:

- Gooder, Eileen. *Latin for local history.* 2nd ed. Longman, 1978.

Appendix 3

SOME TERMS USED IN PROBATE RECORDS

Many technical terms were – and are – used in the process of probate. These are defined here. Definitions given are generally brief, and more information may be given in the main text of this book. Asterisks indicate terms which are defined elsewhere in the glossary, or in the Latin glossary in Appendix 4.

Many archaic and obsolete words can be found in wills and inventories. For a detailed glossary of these, see:

- Raymond, S.A. *Words from wills and other probate records, 1500–1800*. Federation of Family History Societies, 2004.

Account *see* Probate Account

Act Book
The minutes of the probate court, listing probates and administrations granted, and sentences pronounced.

Administration
The right to administer a *decedent's estate.

Administration, Letters of
See Letters of Administration

Administration Bond
A legal document, signed and witnessed, acknowledging the duty to administer an estate, to produce an inventory or accounts, to act as guardian to a minor, or to undertake some other task imposed by the probate court, with a penalty imposed in case of non-performance.

Administrator/Administratrix
Person appointed by the *probate court to administer an *intestate's estate, or to replace an *executor who had renounced the position. Normally the next of kin, or perhaps the leading creditor.

Admon
Abbreviation for *administration bond.

Advocate
In church courts, the professional lawyer who pleads on behalf of a litigant.

Affidavit
A written statement, confirmed by *oath, and used as evidence in court.

Affinity
Relationship through marriage rather than blood.

Affirmation
A solemn declaration made by a person who refuses to take an *oath for conscientious reasons.

Allegation
The plaintiff's pleading in a law suit.

Annuity
An amount paid to the recipient regularly – originally annually.

Answer
The defendant's response to the plaintiff's *allegation, or to an *interrogatory.

Appeal
Application to a superior court to alter a judgement made in a lower court.

Appraiser
Person who values a probate inventory. Sometimes known as a 'praiser'.

Archdeacon
An ecclesiastical officer next in rank to the bishop, usually possessing administrative authority over an *archdeaconry.

Archdeaconry
The area under the jurisdiction of an *archdeacon; the lowest ecclesiastical court.

Arches, Court of
See Court of Arches

Assizes
Courts presided over by judges drawn from the central courts, which went on circuit to supervise *Quarter Sessions.

Attested
Sworn

Beneficiary
In probate records, the *legatee.

Bequeath
To give one's goods away by will.

Bequest
Goods and property left by will; a legacy.

Bishop
A senior clergyman, who exercises authority over a diocese.

Bishops' Registers
In the medieval period, these included a wide range of letters and other documents, including wills. They are not to be confused with *will registers.

Bond
See Administration Bond

British Record Society
See Index Library

Calendar
1. Until 2 September 1752, one of the standard measurements of time in England and Wales was the Julian calendar. On conversion to the Gregorian calendar, eleven days were 'lost', and the calendar recommenced on 14 September. At the same time, the old custom of commencing the year on 25 March was abandoned, and 1 January became the first day of the year.
2. A list of documents, sometimes including abstracts or even full transcripts, but sometimes simply an index.

Calendar of Confirmations and Inventories
Annual listing of Scottish confirmations from 1876 to 1984, held by the National Archives of Scotland.

Canon Law
The law of the church.

Cause
A legal case or lawsuit.

Caveat
A legal process to suspend proceedings until objections have been heard; a notice warning interested parties that a will is to be disputed.

Chancellor
A bishop's senior law officer, who served as his *surrogate, and usually presided as *official principal in the *Consistory Court.

Chancery
See Courts of Equity

Charge
In probate accounts, the amount that the accountant has to account for – normally the amount of the inventory.

Chattel Lease
See Lease

Chattels
Moveable goods, including leases, but excluding *realty.

Citation
A summons to appear before a court so that a case can be heard.

Codicil
An addendum to a will, changing, and perhaps adding, to its provisions. It should be properly signed and witnessed.

Commissariot
In Scotland, the area within the jurisdiction of a Commissary Court. Boundaries were usually based on those of medieval dioceses until 1823; thereafter, they were based on *sheriffdoms.

Commissary
Official appointed to exercise jurisdiction in place of an archbishop, bishop, or other dignitary. In Scotland, the secular judge in a probate court.

Commissary Court
A court acting with delegated powers from a bishop, normally in an *archdeaconry. Common in large dioceses, where the powers of Consistory Courts were delegated to commissary courts. In Scotland, these courts were secular from 1560, and are sometimes referred to as Commissariot Courts. Their powers were transferred to *sheriff's courts after 1824, but the term *commissary court' continued to be used in some instances.

Commission
A document conferring authority, frequently on a local clergyman, to undertake a specific task, e.g. to hear the oaths of executors and administrators, to administer *interrogatories.

Common Law
The secular law of England, based on custom and precedent, which partially governed the descent of *realty.

Common Law Courts
These included Common Pleas, the Exchequer of Pleas, and the King's Bench. They all had jurisdiction over the inheritance of *realty, and hence cases concerning probate could come before them.

Common Pleas
See Common Law Courts

Confirmation
In Scotland, the ratification by a probate court of the testamentary appointment of an executor.

Consanguinity
Blood relationship

Consistory Court
The *bishop's own court, which had superior *jurisdiction in the *diocese, and could hear appeals from the judgements of *archdeaconry courts. When the *bishop undertook a visitation, the powers of the *archdeaconry court were *inhibited in favour of the Consistory Court. Sometimes its powers were delegated to *Commissary Courts.

Contumacy
Contempt of court, shown by a failure to appear when cited.

Coparcenor
A person who jointly inherits an estate.

Copyhold
A type of land tenure in which the tenant held by copy of court roll.

Court for the Probate of Wills and Granting of Administrations
The Interregnum probate court, which replaced PCC and all other probate courts during the period 1653–60.

Court of Arches
The court of the Archbishop of Canterbury, which (amongst other matters) heard *appeals relating to probate business.

Court of Chancery
See Equity Courts

Court of Exchequer
See Equity Courts

Court of Common Pleas
See Common Law Courts

Court of Session
The supreme court in Scotland, which had superior jurisdiction over probate.

Coverture
The legal status of a married woman: all her property was her husband's.

Curator
*Guardian appointed by the probate court over minors under twenty-one but over fourteen (boys) or twelve (girls).

Dean & Chapter
Cathedral dignitaries who frequently held *peculiar jurisdiction over particular parishes.

Death Duties
Collective name for *estate duty, *legacy duty, and *succession duty, levied on *decedents' estates from 1780.

Decedent
The deceased.

Decree
The sentence or final judgement of a court.

Defendant
The accused in a court of law.

Deponent
Witness.

Deposition
Evidence given to a court under oath.

Desperate Debt
A debt for which there is no bond, and which therefore may be difficult to recover.

Devise
To leave *realty by will. Sometimes used more widely, in place of *bequeath.

Diocese
The area under the authority of a bishop.

Discharge
In probate accounts, the payments made by the executor or administrator.

Doctors Commons
This was a College for civil (ecclesiastical) lawyers, where the *PCC, the *Court of Arches, the Consistory Court of the Bishop of London, and other courts, met and kept their records.

Equity
General legal principles which modified the application of the *common law, ensuring that judgements were given equitably.

Equity Courts
These included the Court of Chancery, the Court of Exchequer, the Court of Requests, and the Court of Star Chamber. All had some *jurisdiction over the inheritance of *realty, and hence cases concerning *probate came before them.

Estate
Assets, including both *chattels and *realty.

Estate Duty
A type of *death duty, levied from 1894 to 1976 on both moveable property and *realty.

Examination
The questioning of a witness in court.

Exchequer, Court of
See Equity Courts

Exchequer of Pleas
See Common Law Courts

Executor/Executrix
The person(s) appointed by a testator to carry out the provisions of his/her will, and to administer the estate. There could be more than one.

Exhibit
A document or other item used as evidence in court.

Exor
Abbreviation for executor or executrix.

Folio
Individual leaf of paper or parchment (either loose or bound), numbered in a series on its front (*recto) only.

Freehold
A type of land tenure, conferring absolute ownership under the Crown.

Grant of Administration
See Letters of Administration

Grant of Probate
The formal acknowledgement by a *probate court of the genuineness of a *will, and of the right of the named *executor to administer the *estate. The grant is usually noted on the *verso of original wills, and at the foot of *registered wills, as well as being recorded in *act books where they were kept.

Guardian
See also *Curator and *Tuition. A person legally appointed in stand *in loco parentis* for a minor, or to administer the property of others deemed incapable of managing their own affairs. Children over the age of seven were permitted to choose their own guardians.

Heritable Property
In Scotland, *realty, which could not be bequeathed by will until 1868.

High Court of Delegates
The court of appeal for the *PCC and other church courts, operative from 1532 until 1833.

Holographic Will
A *will written solely by the *testator. It required three witnesses.

Index
An alphabetical list of entries in documents, indicating where individual items can be found.

Index Library
A series of *indexes to (mainly) probate records, published by the British Record Society.

Inhibition
The suspension of the authority of a court during the visitation of the bishop or archbishop.

Instance Case
A case heard in court at the instance of an interested party, rather than by direction of the court.

Interlocutory Decree
A temporary judgement made by a court that can be revoked if more information, e.g. a *will, is discovered.

Interrogatory
Written questions prepared by a litigant and put to witnesses.

Intestate
A person who died without leaving a valid will.

Intimation
A warning issued to a party who has failed to appear in court when summoned.

Inventory
See Probate Inventory

Judicial Committee of the Privy Council
The court of appeal for the *PCC 1834–58.

Jurat
The final statement of an *affidavit, naming its author, and giving the place where it was made, and the name of the person before whom it was made.

Jurisdiction
The power of a court over particular matters and places.

King's Bench
See Common Law Courts

Lease
A deed by which *realty is held by a tenant from a landowner, normally for rent, for a specified term. Such leases were considered to be *chattels, not *realty, and hence *bequests of them were subject to the *jurisdiction of ecclesiastical *probate courts.

Legacy
See Bequest

Legacy Duty
A tax imposed on legacies and *residues of personal estates between 1780 and 1949. Registers survive from 1796 only.

Legatee
The person who benefits from a will; the beneficiary.

Letters of Administration
The formal document by which a *probate court granted authority to an *administrator (usually the next of kin, or perhaps the leading creditor) to administrate an *intestate *estate. These letters were given to administrators. They do not normally survive, but their issue may be recorded in *act books.

Limited Administration/Probate
A grant of *administration or *probate limited to a specific period, or to a specific portion of the *estate.

Manor
The area over which a manorial lord claimed the right to hold courts. Very occasionally, these courts exercised *probate *jurisdiction.

Ministrant
*Defendant.

Moiety
A half share.

Monition
A notice requiring a person to appear before a court, and to produce specific documents.

Moveable Property
In Scotland, *personalty.

Nuncupative Will
A will made orally on the death-bed in the presence of *witnesses, but not written down at the time, nor signed by the *testator.

172

Oath
A promise to tell the truth, sworn on a Bible.

Official Principal
The deputy to a *bishop or *archdeacon, who actually conducted the *probate court.

PCC
Abbreviation frequently used for the *Prerogative Court of Canterbury

PCY
Abbreviation frequently used for the *Prerogative Court of York.

Parish
The area served by a rector or vicar.

Party
Participants in a deed, or in litigation.

Peculiar
An area outside of the normal ecclesiastical *jurisdiction of the diocesan *bishop and/or the *archdeacon. Jurisdiction over them could be held by other bishops, by *Deans and Chapters, by the Crown, by manorial lords, or by some other institution or dignitary.

Personalty
Possessions such as *chattels, money, credits, and leases, subject to the jurisdiction of ecclesiastical probate courts when left by *will.

Plaintiff
The *party who brings a legal action. Also known as a promoter in ecclesiastical courts.

Praiser
See Appraiser

Prebend
The property which provided an income for a member of a Cathedral Chapter. Sometimes, this included *probate *jurisdiction over a *peculiar.

Prebendary
The holder of a *prebend.

Prerogative Courts
The principal probate courts of the Archbishops of Canterbury, York, and Armagh, which exercised superior jurisdiction over their *provinces.

Primogeniture
The system of inheritance in which *realty descends to the eldest son.

Probate
The official recognition of the legal validity of a will; the process of proving it.

Probate Account
The account which an executor or administrator was sometimes required to exhibit. It showed his expenditure, and the manner in which he had distributed the *estate.

Probate Courts
The courts in which *wills were proved, and *administrations granted. Until 1858, they were usually, but not always, ecclesiastical courts.

Probate Inventory
List of *chattels left by a *decedent, with appraised values.

Proctor
A lawyer in an ecclesiastical court.

Promoter
See Plaintiff

Proved
A *will which has been formally accepted by a *probate court as genuine, and for which the executor has been granted *probate.

Province
The area under the jurisdiction of an archbishop.

Proxy
Person acting on behalf of another; document appointing a *proctor to act as proxy.

Quarter Sessions
The quarterly meeting of Justices of the Peace, which governed each county, and exercised judicial powers.

Realty, Real Estate, Real Property
Lands and buildings held *freehold. Realty was not under the *jurisdiction of ecclesiastical courts.

Registered Wills
See Will Registers

Registry
The office of the diocesan registrar, where records (including wills) were kept.

Relict
The widow of a testator.

Renunciation
The action of the person named as *executor when he/she declines to accept the responsibility; the document by which the renunciation is made.

Resealed
Grant of probate or administration made by an English court and copied to its opposite number in Scotland, or vice versa. It enabled succession to the property of decedents who had lived in one jurisdiction, but held property in the other.

Residuary Devisee
The heir who inherits the residue of *realty after all debts and charges on that property have been paid.

Residuary Legatee
The *legatee who takes the *residue of a *testator's *estate after the payment of all other legacies and other debts. Usually also the *executor/executrix.

Residue
The remainder of an estate after all legacies have been met. Frequently bequeathed to *executors.

Respondent
One who answers; the *defendant.

Retours
In Scotland, returns made by juries called to determine the right of vassals to inherit landed property.

Reversionary Interest
An interest in *realty that reverts to its grantee or his heirs after a specific period of time, or when its holder dies.

Right Heirs
Heirs at law if the provisions of a will are ineffective, e.g. if a *beneficiary is dead.

Seat
One of the five administrative divisions into which the business of the PCC was divided after 1719.

See
The seat of a bishop.

Sentence
The final judgement in a cause, frequently entered in an *act book.

Sheriff's Court
In Scotland, the court which has exercised *probate *jurisdiction since 1824. The term *'commissary court' sometimes continued to be used for this court.

Sheriffdom
The area over which a Scottish *Sheriff's Court exercised *jurisdiction from 1824. Originally, their boundaries roughly coincided with county boundaries, but now each sheriffdom covers a wider area.

Sperate Debt
A recoverable debt. Contrast *desperate debt.

Star Chamber
See Equity Courts

Succession Duty
A tax imposed on the inheritance of *realty between 1853 and 1949.

Surrogate
An official acting in a judicial capacity as a deputy to a *bishop, archbishop, or *archdeacon.

Testament
A term used from the sixteenth century interchangeably with *will, but originally referring to a document concerned with the disposition of *personalty only.

Testament Dative
The documents drawn up by Scottish Commissary Courts where the *decedent had not left a will.

Testament Testamentar
The documents drawn up by Scottish Commissary Courts where the *decedent had left a will.

Testator/Testatrix
The maker of a will.

Trustees/Trusts
A group of individuals appointed by will or other deed to hold the grantee's property jointly in trust, with instructions to apply its income for specific purposes.

Tuition
Guardianship of orphaned minors aged under fifteen (boys) or thirteen (girls).

Tuition bond
The *administration bond by which a guardian guaranteed the performance of his duties.

Tutor
See *Guardian

Vacancy
Technically, when a bishop or other official died or resigned, his court was inhibited, and its business carried on in a superior court. This was often 'pro forma' only, as the officials of the lower court simply carried on their work in the name of the superior court.

Visitation
Systematic inquiry by a *bishop or *archdeacon into the state of his diocese or archdeaconry. During the visitation, the activities of the courts affected would be under *inhibition.

Warrant
See Commission

Will
Originally a document bequeathing *realty only. The term's meaning was widened from the sixteenth century to include the bequest of *personalty. In Scotland, the term *testament continued to be used until 1868, since it was not legally possible to bequeath realty in that country.

Will Register
Register of a *probate court in which proved *wills are copied by court officials. The term should not be confused with the *bishop's register.

Witness

A person who sees a testator making his will, or who is called to give evidence before a court.

Writ

A document conveying either a royal command, or an order from a court.

LATIN GLOSSARY

Asterisks indicate terms defined in Appendix 3.

Amita
Father's sister

Attestation
*Affidavit

Bona
Goods

Bona Notabilia
Literally, considerable goods; legally, those worth more than £5. If a *testator had bona notabilia in more than one *jurisdiction, his will had to be proved in a superior court.

Bona Paraphernalia
The personal goods of a widow, other than her dowry, e.g. clothes and jewellery.

Bona Vacantia
The goods of an intestate who has no known heirs.

Breve
*Writ

Comitatus
County

Compos Mentis
Of sound mind

Coram
Before

Denarius
Penny

Dominus
Lord, master, sir.

Eodem die
The same day

Episcopus
*Bishop.

Feme covert
Married woman

Feme sole
Unmarried woman

Filia
Daughter

Filius
Son

Frater
Brother

Heres
Heir

Imperpetuum
In perpetuity

Imprimis
In the first place.

In partibus transmarinis
Overseas, abroad.

Infra
Below

Inter alia
Amongst other things

Judex
Judge

Lego
I bequeath

Liberi
Children

Libra
Pound

Maritus
Husband

Mater
Mother

Mater tera
Mother's sister, aunt

Medietas
*Moiety.

Nepos
Nephew

Neptis
Niece

Nuper
Late, lately.

Nurus
Daughter in law

Obsequia
Funeral rites.

Para rationalibus
A reasonable portion

Pater
Father

Patruus
Father's brother, uncle

Probo
I prove

Quietus est
All is quiet – the accountant is absolved of any further responsibility for the estate.

Recto
The right-hand page of an open book; the front of a leaf of paper or parchment.

Relicte dicti defuncti
Widow of the said deceased

Residuum
*Residue, remainder.

Sede Vacantia
During the vacancy (with reference to the period between the death of a bishop or archdeacon, and the induction of his replacement).

Solidus
Shilling

Sororius
Sister's husband or son

Sponsa
Wife

Sponsus
Husband

Spurius
Illegitimate

Susceptorus
Godparent

Terra
Land

Ultra
Above

Uxor
Wife

Uxoratus
Married man

Vacatur
Void

Verso
The left-hand page of an open book; the back of a leaf of paper or parchment.

Appendix 5

LEGISLATION AFFECTING PROBATE

The content of probate records depended upon what the law required. The law evolved over time, and it is therefore desirable to be aware of the various statutes that were passed, and their implications for the records. Brief details of the more important statutes are given below; the actual text of these and a variety of other relevant statutes can be read at:

- Durham University: Probate Legislation **http://familyrecords.dur. ac.uk/nei/NEI_law.htm**

The statutes are also, of course, available in a printed edition, which is widely available:

- Raithby, John, ed. *Statutes of the Realm*. 12 vols. Record Commission, 1810–28.

*c.*1072: **Ordinance separating Spiritual and Temporal Courts**

William I removed spiritual pleas from the jurisdiction of the temporal Hundred courts, and laid the basis for the system of ecclesiastical courts which later developed into probate courts.

1225: **Magna Carta**

King John granted the supervision of intestates' estates to the church.

1357: **Administration of Intestates Goods (31 Edward III c.11)**

The probate courts were required to grant the administration of the goods of intestates to 'the next and most lawful friends' of the deceased. The administrator was to have the same powers as an executor.

1529: **What Fees Ought to be Taken for Probate of Testaments (21 Henry VIII c.5)**

This Act laid down the maximum scale of fees which could be charged by probate officials. Fees depended on the value of decedents' estates. Nothing could be charged on estates valued at under £5. Estates valued under £10 could be charged 3s 6d. The maximum fee chargeable was 5/–. Executors and administrators were required to find appraisers willing to compile an inventory; this had to be in duplicate, and indented; one copy was to be retained, and the other was to be exhibited in court.

It was also laid down that the administration of intestates was to be granted firstly to widows, or to next of kin at the discretion of the court.

1540: Statute of Wills (33 Henry VIII, c.1)

Under this Act, the former prohibition on the devise of lands in wills was abolished (apart from certain restrictions on land held directly from the Crown). Landed property could be devised in wills, although jurisdiction over such devises remained with the secular courts, and not with ecclesiastical probate courts. The Crown retained its right to feudal dues from lands devised.

1609: Shop Book Evidence (7 Jas I, c.12)

Traders who had sold goods on credit, and recorded them in their shop books, could only recover such debts if they were claimed within twelve months of their being incurred.

1644: Ordinance Claiming Parliamentary Control of the Prerogative Court of Canterbury

This Parliamentary Ordinance authorised Sir Nathanael Brent to continue the work of the PCC under Parliamentary auspices during the Civil War.

1653: An Act for Probate of Wills, and granting Administrations

This act established the Interregnum Court of Probate, which replaced all ecclesiastical probate courts until the Restoration in 1660.

1670: Act for Better Settling of Intestates' Estates (22–3 Chas I, c.10)

Popularly known as the Statute of Distribution, this act authorized the judges of probate courts to take bonds from administrators, and established a set form of words to be used in them. After the payment of debts, a third of estates was to be granted to widows. The residue was to be distributed equally between children. Any child who had already received an estate from the deceased (other than estate descending by primogeniture) was to be excluded. An account was to be exhibited at a given date, usually within two years. The act was renewed twice, and made permanent in 1685.

1676: Act for Prevention of Fraud & Perjuries (29 Car. 2, c.3)

Nuncupative wills for estates valued at over £30 were required to have at least three witnesses. They had to be proved within six months, unless it could be shown that they had been written down within six days. However, they could not be proved within fourteen days of the testator's death, and the widow and next of kin had to be given an opportunity to dispute the will. The act did not affect wills made by soldiers and seamen on active service for the Crown.

1685: Act for Reviving and Continuance of Several Acts of Parliament (4 William & Mary, c.2)

The probate clause of this act laid down that, in future, probate accounts were only to be required if demanded by representatives of a minor, by creditors, or by the next of kin.

1692: Revocation of the Custom of the Province of York (4 William & Mary, c.2)

This Act abolished the customary rights of widows and children in the Province of York to a share in the estates of decedents, and gave testators in that Province the same rights to dispose of their property as those enjoyed by inhabitants of the Province of Canterbury.

1695: Revocation of the Custom of Wales (7 & 8 William III, c.38)

This Act did for Wales what the 1692 act did for the Province of York.

1703: West Riding Deeds Registry Act (2 & 3 Anne, c.4)

The West Riding Deeds Registry was established. Deeds (including wills devising lands) were to be registered in the West Riding.

1707: East Riding Deeds Registry Act (6 Anne, c.62)

The East Riding Deeds Registry was established.

1708: Middlesex Deeds Registry Act (7 Anne, c.20)

A deeds registry for Middlesex was established.

1716: Registration of Papist Deeds Act (3 George I, c.18)

Wills of Roman Catholics devising lands had to be registered in either a central or a local court.

1734: North Riding Deeds Registry Act (8 George II, c.6)

A deeds registry for the North Riding was established.

1751: Attestation of Wills Act (25 George II, c.6)

Beneficiaries of wills could not witness them without forfeiting their right to legacies. Creditors, however, could.

1780: Legacy Duty Act (20 George III, c.28)

Legacy duty was first imposed.

1796: Legacy Duty Act (36 George III, c.52)

By this Act, a duty was made payable on legacies, and on the residues of estates of the deceased. Assessment was based on probate records. Liability for this duty was subsequently extended by the Legacy Duty Act 1805 (45 George III, c.28), and by the Stamp Act 1815 (55 George III, c.184)

1837: Wills Act (7 William IV & 1 Victoria, c.26)

This Act removed all remaining restrictions on what could be left by will. However, wills could only be made by adults aged over twenty-one (except married women), and had to be in writing. Nuncupative wills ceased to be valid. There had to be at least two witnesses, and any bequests made to witnesses were void. Creditors, however, could be witnesses without prejudicing the money owed to them. Marriage automatically revoked a will.

Wills made by soldiers or sailors on active service were not affected by the Act.

1853: Succession Duty Act (16 & 17 Victoria c.51)

The Legacy Duty Act of 1796 was amended by this Act, which imposed succession duty.

1857: Probate Act (20 & 21 Victoria c.77)

This Act dissolved all pre-existing probate courts, both ecclesiastical and lay, and established a single Probate Court, with forty district registries. See Chapter 7 above.

1868: Titles to Land Consolidation (Scotland) Act (31 & 32 Victoria. c.101)

Scottish testators were authorised to bequeath realty by will.

1882: Married Womens Property Act (45 & 46 Victoria c.75)

Married women were granted the right to hold property in their own names, and to dispose of it by will, without requiring permission from their husbands.

SUBJECT INDEX

PLACE NAME INDEX

Please note that this index does not include place names in appendix 2, as these are listed alphabetically by county.

PERSONAL NAME INDEX